Children's Serm

G000124952

COME as a CHILD 2

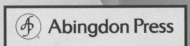
Abingdon Press

Indexes: Scripture • Key Word • Lectionary

COME AS A CHILD
CHILDREN'S SERMONS TO SEE AND HEAR, 2

ISBN: 0-687-04584-3

02 03 04 05 06 07 08 09 10 11—10 9 8 7 6 5 4 3 2 1

MANUFACTURED IN THE UNITED STATES OF AMERICA

CONTENTS

Introduction

The Stories

Indexes

INTRODUCTION

Let Me Tell You a Story: The Oral Tradition in Biblical History

We've spent a lot of time around the campfire with friends or family or with coworkers. Sometimes the campfire is a planned affair, with an emcee going through a list of skits and songs presented by various participants. Sometimes there is no program, and the campfire is just a bunch of us sitting around on lawn chairs, tree stumps, or blankets. There is often hot chocolate. There is often popcorn or chips. There is always singing. And there are always a lot of stories. We camp with friends whose relationships with us go way back. These are people we've known since elementary school. As friends and families we have traveled, schooled, canoed, camped, married, loaned, birthed, consoled, feasted . . . experienced life and lives.

We know a lot about these friends and their families. They know a lot about us. So when the campfire time turns to storytelling, a lot of the stories are the old and ancient tales of our high school pranks or our daring wilderness adventures. These are stories we've all heard a million times before. Even the people present who were not around for the actual experience have heard the stories a million times before. No one seems to mind hearing it again.

A few new stories are introduced each year, because life continues apart from one another and there are things to catch up on. And every now and then there is a new person in the group — a spouse or a child — and his or her stories get added to the mix.

This is how we imagine communities have worked for a few millennia, before the advent of printing presses, celluloid film, and binary transmission. We have an image of the evening meal being shared by a group of families around a fire on the plains or in a cave or in a thatched longhouse. It would have been a time when the community came together and told the stories of what had happened during the day. The community would catch up on things; but then the storytelling would shift to the old and ancient tales of the ancestors, and perhaps one or two especially gifted speakers would be asked to recount a well-loved yarn of the gods or of the netherworld. The listeners would laugh at the funny spots, weep at the sad spots, and bulge eyes at the suspenseful spots, just like we do the right things at the right spots in the movie theatres.

This was how the knowledge of the race of humans was passed down through time. They told the stories of the things they knew: their history, their culture, and their faith. To a large extent this was how the knowledge of our religious faith has made it to us in the twenty-first century. Most of the stories and the history we enjoy from the Old and New Testaments came through a long period of sharing around a fire or in small groups, until the stories were committed to a written form to be preserved in a formal version.

Now we are asking you to continue this well-respected form of faith sharing. There are plenty of books. There are enough movies. We can get more information than we need from the Internet. While all these media are valuable in their own ways, we want to promote a method that young and old can all grasp.

We want you to tell a story. Each Sunday in church a group of young children gather at the front of our churches to hear the worship leader tell them about God. While the time is there for the children, the adults are listening in from the pews. The relatively new tradition of the storytime for children in worship service offers us the opportunity to employ the ancient tradition of oral transmission of our faith stories. Use this time well. Use the modern and advanced technologies available to us to develop and prepare meaningful worship. But remember that through the oral sharing of our lives, our faith, and our God, we are connected to a practice reaching far back into the history of time when God first started sharing God's self with us.

When Good Stories Go Bad

Reggie Jackson, Jose Canseco, Mickey Mantle — for those who know baseball, you'll recognize the names of three ballplayers who can really hit. All three are among the top ten home run hitters of all time. Jackson hit 563 home runs in 2,820 games; Mantle hit 536 in 2,401 games; and Jose Canseco, (who, as of the writing of this book, is still an active player in major league baseball), has hit 462 home runs in 1,887 games. That's pretty impressive, but even more so are some other statistics they have amassed in their careers. Most notably, these three — Jackson, Canseco, and Mantle — are ranked first, second, and third in the all-time strikeout category.

While on the one hand this might be seen as a dubious distinction, racking up those strikeouts means two things: you had a lot of bats, and someone had the confidence to put you in the game, even though you struck out a lot. A manager isn't going to send a ballplayer to the plate more than two thousand times if it's going to hurt the team. These three ballplayers proved they could help the team; they could swing for the seats and do it. Jose Canseco holds the distinction of being the only ballplayer to hit a baseball into the 500-level of the Toronto Skydome! In trying to knock the ball out of the park, they knew when they stepped up to the plate that they might strike out. That's part of the game. You can't hit a home run in every turn at bat. On the other hand, you can't win a game in one swing if the bat never leaves your shoulder.

If you're going to hit home runs, you're also going to strike out. It's true in baseball; it's true in love; it's true in everything, including story-telling. Every time you take the risk of telling a story, or illustrating your sermon by hunkering down at the front of your church with an odd toy or picture or tale, you take a risk (for more on risk see our stories for Pentecost 11 and 25). You may find the perfect way to bring your message into absolute clarity, and hear the equivalent of the roar of the crowd, "Aha!" Or you may hear the hush of the stadium as everyone wonders why you swung at a pitch over your head. That is the chance you take.

However, remember Reggie Jackson struck out 4.6 times for every home run he hit. And it's the home runs that stick out in our minds.

Therefore, the question is not whether you will bomb, but what you'll do with the moment when it happens. Here, the most important quality you can possess is humility. We could take the approach that God uses us to bring a message to the congregation; and we need to remember that sometimes the message we have in mind is not the one God has in mind, and that sometimes God uses children to bring down the mighty. While we won't argue that this never happens, our guess is that more often than not it is simply a function of Murphy's Law: "If something can go wrong, it will."

When working with children it's important to remember two rules:

1. Guard the microphone with your life.

As with e-mail, once something enters the system, you can't get it back, no matter how hard you try.

2. Beware the open-ended question.

Although there are times when you may want to throw a question out to the children, be careful. You can't control their response.

Once, Jim was trying to demonstrate that just because we want to hear something, that doesn't mean it is right or good for us, and so the story worked like this:

Jim gathered the kids together and then pulled out a newspaper. He started reading phony stories from the paper, revealing recent research that should make the kids really happy. The news items included: "Chocolate bars are good for you; you should eat three a day." "Going to bed early is bad for kids; they need to stay up as late as they want for maximum alertness." You get the idea. Finally Jim read, "Going to school and doing homework impairs a child's natural intelligence. Children should be kept out of school and allowed to play and watch television every day."

In the discussion that followed, the kids admitted that although they would like to hear those things, they knew they were not true, nor were they good for them. Feeling a certain amount of success and pride, Jim started letting the microphone out, giving the children a chance to voice their wisdom to the congregation.

"And what would happen if you never went to school?" Jim asked. "What kind of a job would you get? How would you make a living?" At this point Jared, Jim's son, leaned into the microphone and chimed in, "I could get a job if I didn't go to school." Now confronted by the challenge Jim stepped into the maws of danger, "Jared," he asked, "how could you get a job if you didn't go to school?" "I'd write stories," he replied. "You don't have to know anything to do that."

At this point the entire congregation burst into laughter. There was no point in trying to recover. Any attempt at explanation would have become too bogged down and "preachy." The whole moment would have gone into a tailspin. The children would not have understood it, and the rest of the congregation would have been left staring at a drowning man clawing and struggling against the tide.

Losing the story is not always a disaster; in fact, our experience has been that it's almost never a disaster. Remember, the children's story is a part of the worship service. We pray for the Holy Spirit to lead when we plan and participate in worship. Sometimes we need to trust more in the Spirit than in our own abilities. If you tell enough stories, occasionally a few will go bad on you. It's not like it hasn't happened with the occasional sermon. So our advice is: expect it, accept it, and then revel in it.

Stories We Ought to Tell

Author Ralph Milton relates the following in his book *Angels in Red Suspenders*:

"When my Mennonite grandparents settled in the inhospitable west, they found every excuse available to gather together with their neighbors. They told stories and cracked sunflower seeds until the floor was an inch deep in husks. The seeds were high in calories (which they didn't know) and the stories were high in community building (which they felt). It was these stories that helped them know who they were, why they were out there on the cold windy prairie shivering in sod huts, and what their dreams were.

"The stories were the fabric that held that Mennonite society together, and communicated to their children and their grandchildren who they were, and what was right and wrong and valuable. In the stories, far more than in the church, they communicated their real understanding of God. It's stories told while eating sunflower seeds that communicate who we really are and what we really believe." (Paraphrased from *Angels in Red Suspenders*, published by Northstone Publishing. Used by permission. Available at Wood Lake books, 1-800-663-2775.)

What the preacher says is merely commentary. Amen.

Stories are told again and again to define who we are and what we believe. We must tell them. Now, there are many stories we like to tell. Everyone has his or her favorite. We need to tell the stories repeatedly. And we need to tell all of them. The stories that define us are not just the ones with the funny or happy ending. We need to tell the good, the bad, and the ugly, because we are all those things. As Milton says, "The stories were the fabric that held that Mennonite society together." Fabric has a lot of different threads, colors and textures.

We need to be brave enough to incorporate all of our beliefs into the stories and sermon illustrations we use in a worship service. Remember that the children's story is an integral part of the worship service. That means that it has relevance to everything that encapsulates it and to everyone who participates in it or listens to it. This is not a time to sugarcoat biblical truths or social reality. This is one of the best vehicles to do this. Often you can slide something into the moments with the children in your church that the adults need to hear, but won't accept if it is told forthright.

There was a young youth pastor at a church in western Canada who decided that many people in his congregation approached Sunday morning worship with a demeanor less than worthy of a people who stood side by side to bask in God's grace and celebrate God's love. He looked out at the sour faces, mouths drawn into frowns that looked painful even. He braced himself, with one hand on each side of the pulpit, and he intoned, "I have never seen such long faces in a house of worship in my life. Why, some of you people could suck a corn cob out of a gopher hole without bending your knees." This story is now listed among those that one tells on his or her last day at a church. You know the kind we mean, all those sermons that you've got filed away to preach when the folks in the pews have no more control over your salary or your pension.

Stories have often been used to communicate very deep and powerful ideas. Parables enabled Jesus to communicate complex and lofty ideals in a way that even we could understand. Nathan used the same method with King David. Human history is rife with examples of stories being used in this way. Do not be afraid to tuck a little something extra for your congregation into the children's story. The best of stories, in our experience, are those that have cross-generational appeal. Just think about your favorite animated films: They have a storyline and humor geared to the younger set, while also providing the parents with enough humor and story to make the movie interesting for them. When they are at their best, these animated films deal with profound meaning in a way that makes it accessible to all viewers.

Should the goal of our worship services be any less?

Sometimes we come up with an idea for an illustration and wonder if we have the guts to pull it off in the worship service. We admit to having done some pretty daring things in the children's time of worship, and you will probably find a few stories in this series that you are hesitant to perform in your church. Consider, for example, the story of Telemachus that we have for Pentecost 7. It is a disturbing story for adults, let alone children, and we won't be surprised that many readers will not use it. We included it in this book, though, because we believe it is a challenging theme and a challenging illustration.

Should you use this story? We're not there behind you to tell you that everything will be all right if you try something complicated or risky in the children's time, and it backfires. We can only promise you these stories have all been done at church by one of us. You have to be the judge of your own situation. When we are uncertain about one of our ideas, we usually get over it with the conviction that gospel is a risk. We never see ourselves as called to go the easy route to something like a cross.

Having said that about some of our illustrations, imagine how we might agonize over some of the themes we wish to address in the children's time. We'd like to get the point across to the children that not all things in the church are perfect. Some Christians do not act Christian even in your church. Sometimes we'd like to say the church is wrong. Sometimes we'd like to say our church has to do more. Do we dare dream up an illustration that will definitely unsettle the establishment of the church? The children's story should not become a soapbox for your personal agenda, but we should be bold enough to use the children's story to challenge as well as to educate. We mentioned earlier a young pastor at a church in western Canada. Could he have made his point more effectively using an illustration?

Here again, the authors are not there with you to tell you everything will go well. Everything can't be expected to go well when we stick out our necks for what we believe, in a culture that believes differently. We all know that. So here is a challenge. Do you dare dream up an illustration or a theme that will challenge or threaten the establishment of your church? Let us know how it works out.

Season of Advent

Isaiah
64:1-9

Psalm
80:1-7,
17-19

1 Corinthians
1:3-9

Mark
13:24-37

Keywords

Advent
Calendars
Gifts
Hope
Waiting

Message

The Lord is coming to set the world right. We do not know when. We wait and prepare so that we are ready.

Commentary

The Advent season is set apart by the church as a waiting time. Waiting for what? Waiting for God to make God's presence known in our world. Since the birth of Christ, we know that God's presence on earth occurred with Jesus the Son and continues forever through the Holy Spirit. The lectionary readings for this Sunday dwell on this idea of God coming to the earth to set things right. It is a message of hope to a world that seems to know that it cannot make things right on its own. The world needs divine intervention.

Isaiah and Psalm 80 both use images of a world gone bad: "We have all become like one who is unclean, and all our righteous deeds are like a filthy cloth" (Isaiah 64:6). "How long will you be angry with your people's prayers?" (Psalm 80:4). But both selections end with a call for God to come and set things right.

The passage in First Corinthians stresses that God has enriched us all. We are lacking in nothing. "[God] will also strengthen you to the end, so that you may be blameless . . ." (1 Corinthians 1:8). It is God who will save us.

Jesus prophesied in Mark about the coming of the Lord, and this was accompanied by angels who "gather [God's] elect" to be saved. Again, the initiative to save is God's. Jesus then cautioned his listeners about the advent of this occasion. No one knows the date or the hour, not even Jesus himself. So what are we to do? Wait and be ready.

These themes are what we work through throughout the Advent season — waiting and preparing so that we are ready for the coming of the Lord.

Story: THE FIRST DAY OF WAITING

For the four Sundays of Advent and for Christmas or Christmas Eve, we will do an integrated series of stories. We start this year off with a lot of preparation; but once this is done, your children's stories are ready for the whole season, and you can worry about other things.

Advent is all about waiting and preparing for the coming gift. We are able to play on this excitement and wonder as we proceed through the series of related children's stories each week. You need five gifts and five boxes in progressive sizes so that they can nest inside one another to make one box. Read through the stories for the whole season in order to prepare these boxes.

Prepare the Christmas/Christmas Eve present in a gift-wrapped box, with a notice or card saying, "Do not open until the Last Day of Waiting." Put this present inside another box along with the presents for Advent 4. Wrap this box and include a card to say, "Do not open until the Fourth Day of Waiting." Put this present inside another box along with the presents for Advent 3. Wrap this box and include a card to say, "Do not open until the Third Day of Waiting." I hope by now you're getting the idea about what to do with Advent 2 and Advent 1.

If everything has been prepared correctly, when the children gather for this story time you will have a rather large wrapped present with a card. Make the card personal for the children, but make sure it says, "Do not open until the First Day of Waiting." Explain that Advent is about waiting and preparing.

Like this present that could not be opened until today, we wait with hope and expectation for God's gift.

Have someone open the gift, but be careful. Once when I did this story, the excited children started ripping into the second gift before I could stop them. In this present there is another present with a notice not to open until the Second Sunday of Advent. There are also Advent calendars for each of the children. If you can afford one for each child to take home, that is best; but it will still work if you get one good-sized one and keep it at the church or in the Sunday school room to be referred to each week.

The calendars are for us to mark the waiting time between now and Christmas, and in this way we build up our hope and expectation for the coming of Christ.

Isaiah
40:1-11

Psalm
85:1-2, 8-13

2 Peter
3:8-15a

Mark 1:1-8

Keywords

Advent

Coupons

John the
Baptist

Promise

Message

We believe in God's promises of a messiah and our deliverance. While time passes before this happens, we see visible signs of the promise.

Commentary

The season of Advent continues, and our readings for this Sunday continue to reflect the themes of waiting for good things.

Isaiah is a familiar passage including, "The grass withers, the flower fades, but the word of our God will stand forever" (Isaiah 40:8). The passage as a whole assures God's people in exile that their suffering is close to an end and that good things are coming to them. There is even the word *reward* used in verse 10, which we will use in today's story. Psalm 85 repeats the idea that because God loves God's people, they will receive good things.

When this will happen will remain a mystery as described in last week's reading from Mark and again in this week's reading from Second Peter. The Lord's time is different from our own, but we are assured that the good things promised will happen in the Lord's time.

Visible signs of this imminent event are described in Mark's Gospel as he describes the ministry of John the Baptist. Mark lifts some of the phrases from Isaiah 40 to make his point. John proclaimed, "The one who is more powerful than I is coming after me . . ." (Mark 1:7). John was not the real thing, but he was a visible sign that the real thing was coming soon after him.

Story: THE SECOND DAY OF WAITING

We are continuing the nested present from last week. In this second gift there should be another gift box with a notice that it is not to be opened until the Third Day of Waiting. There should also be some coupons for something simple such as French fries or a milk shake from a local restaurant. We have found that most of the major fast food chains are willing to give churches a handful of coupons for good purposes like this. It's good publicity for them.

As the children gather, bring forward the gift box with the card on it that says, "Do not open until the Second Day of Waiting." Explain to the children that we believe in God's promises of a messiah and our deliverance, but they may not be seen in our lives for a while. Until we see God on earth as promised, we will always be able to see visible signs of the promise.

Have the gift opened and give a coupon to each of the children. Explain that these coupons are not the real things, like fries or drinks, but they are a promise that you can get the real thing soon.

This is what John the Baptist was like to us. He was not the Christ, but the fact that he did his ministry was a sign that God's promise would soon be filled.

You will need:
Nested gifts
Coupons

Third Sunday of Advent

Message

Jesus is the light of the world.

Commentary

These readings today repeat the notions of good things coming to the people God loves. The psalm is a song of rejoicing in response to deliverance, and First Thessalonians calls us to be in a continual state of rejoicing and prayer. Then the Gospel reading from today parallels the Gospel reading from last week with its focus on John the Baptist's identity. In John's version, though, the image of light is central. John the Baptist came to testify to the light, but he was not the light himself. Going one verse beyond the lectionary passage, there is the sentence that sums up our Advent message clearly: "The true light, which enlightens everyone, was coming into the world" (John 1:9). The message of light is obvious in our world this time of year. Christmas lights and candles are all over the place. We will use this image of light for today's story.

Isaiah 61:1-4, 8-11

Psalm 126

1 Thessalonians 5:16-24

John 1:6-8, 19-28

Keywords

Advent

Candles

John the
Baptist

Light

You will need:
Nested gifts
Candles

Story: THE THIRD DAY OF WAITING

In the third present there is another present with the notice not to open until the Fourth Day of Waiting. There is also a candle for each child. After the gift is opened, explain to the children that today's Bible story is about how John the Baptist told people about Jesus Christ.

It says that Jesus is the light of the world, and you can certainly see a lot of lights around this time of year on our Christmas trees, our stores, and our front windows.

Have each of the children take a candle to be a reminder that the Jesus we look forward to is the light of the world.

Fourth Sunday of Advent

2 Samuel
7:1-11, 16

Psalm
89:1-4,
19-26

Romans
16:25-27

Luke
1:26-38

Message

As great as God is, God appeared on earth as a little baby, just like all of us.

Commentary

This Sunday we read about the angel Gabriel's visit to Mary to announce that she would have a baby — not just any baby, but "the Son of the Most High." In the two birth stories of Jesus that we have in the Bible (Matthew and Luke), we can see a few differences of emphasis. Both writers make note that Jesus descended from King David, and they provide genealogies to back up the claim. It is interesting to note that in Matthew it is Joseph who had the dreams and visions, while in Luke it is Mary who saw the angel. There is no question about the lineage of Joseph as a descendant of King David, but since the child Jesus was conceived by the Holy Spirit, there is the potential for misunderstandings about his ancestry; and hence the Christian claim that Jesus is of the line of David.

The question of parentage must have been a serious bone of contention. Parentage was important to the early societies since so much of their livelihood depended upon land resources, and the passing of property from generation to generation had to be carefully scrutinized. The importance of ancestry appears in the Old Testament readings for this Sunday as well. After God scuttled King David's plans for a temple, God reassured him that, "Your house and your kingdom shall be made sure forever before me . . ." (2 Samuel 7:16). In the psalm the covenant with David is reaffirmed: "I will establish your descendants forever, and build your throne for all generations" (Psalm 89:4).

God makes promises. God made promises to God's people throughout the Old Testament, and in Jesus Christ another promise has been made, while others have been fulfilled. In this Christ Child the Kingdom of David continues forever. In this Christ Child all humanity is drawn into the covenant — we are all part of the family of God.

Keywords
Advent
Babies
Families
Photos

Story: THE FOURTH DAY OF WAITING

In this Sunday's story we have an image of the new covenant represented by the Christ Child. Nothing is newer than a newborn baby. In the fourth present there is another present with a notice not to open until Christmas Eve/Day. Also have a photo album with pictures of babies. If it's possible to have some baby pictures from baptisms or the nursery at your church, that would be very meaningful. Pictures of yourself or your children as babies would work.

Explain that this is the Fourth Day of Waiting.

This is getting really close to the time of the coming of the baby Jesus. (*Talk about some of the things done around a house when a baby is coming.*) **What do you do to prepare for a baby?**

Some of the children probably will have good memories of preparing for a little sister or a little brother to arrive, or maybe they are the little ones in their family. In that case they might have things to say about what their parent did while getting ready for them to arrive.

Those pleasant thoughts and memories of a new baby are the same sort of thoughts we can have with the coming of the baby Jesus.

You will need:
Nested gifts
Baby pictures

Season of Christmas

Isaiah
9:2-7

Psalm 96

Titus
2:11-14

Luke
2:1-20

Keywords
Christmas
Gifts

Message

Jesus Christ is born. God is here on earth. This is God's greatest gift to God's children.

Commentary

There are many options to the lectionary readings for this day, depending upon the time of day or night your church holds services. We have chosen to use the readings the Revised Common Lectionary has for Christmas Eve. To us they seem to hold the most significant images for this celebration. It also seems to us that most churches will prefer a children's story time in the Christmas Eve service rather than the Christmas vigil or morning service.

In the Isaiah passage there is great joy and celebration: "For a child has been born for us . . . and he is named Wonderful Counselor, Mighty God, Everlasting Father, Prince of Peace" (Isaiah 9:6). These are great images to share in a children's time. The psalm repeats the joyous theme of praise to God for the wonderful gift God has given us. Titus bases its exhortation to its readers on the assertion that "the grace of God has appeared" (Titus 2:11). Titus mentions that it is in God's gift that we are redeemed.

But of course, it is the Gospel reading that is the climax of the season and the service. In Luke the birth of Jesus is reported to us with the detail of an educated person who wanted to be certain that we got the facts right. Luke tells of the journey of Mary and Joseph to Bethlehem, then offers only one verse on the actual birth. Following that is an account of the angelic visit to common shepherds, proclaiming the birth of Jesus. The first angel says this baby is born "to you." This is a peculiar phrasing that makes it clear that the birth of the Christ is a gift to the world, not just to a carpenter family.

Story: GOD'S GREATEST GIFT

In this story we finish the series of nested gifts we have been going through this season. In the final present have a small gift for each child. The gift should have some Christmas significance, such as a tree ornament or a star. Perhaps a church craft group could create some small angels. Be creative and meaningful in choosing something for each child to take home as a memento of this Christmas service.

You will need:
Nested gift

We realize this calls for extra resources on your part, because as everyone knows, Christmas services are when you have record attendance at church. Yes, it's more work; but remember, you have to do all this work before the First Sunday of Advent. Just think of how organized and clever you will seem to your congregation when all of their children go home from this service with a special gift. You can thank us later.

With all of the hoopla that seems to accompany our Christmas services, perhaps it's a good idea to keep the message to the children simple and sweet. They will all be excited about Christmas, and most of the service will have meaning to them. Hand out the gifts.

The baby Jesus has come. The gift from God has arrived. Christmas is all about gifts and all about giving. God gave to us, so we give to one another; and this little gift is something for you to remember God's gift of Jesus Christ.

First Sunday After Christmas Day
(A, B, C)

Message

What is different now that Christ has come?

Commentary

These readings for today give promises and then fulfillment about change. Remember that Isaiah 61 and 62 are in a section believed to have been written after the Babylonian exile. The

Isaiah
61:10–62:3

Psalm 148

Galatians
4:4-7

Luke
2:22-40

Keywords
Change
Color
Different
Spoon

people have been redeemed and can come home. Is anything different about God's people after experiencing this soul-wrenching time? Isaiah says yes. It is compared to a wedding with bride and groom decorated to celebrate a whole new life together. They shall even "be called by a new name that the mouth of the LORD will give" (Isaiah 62:2).

The Galatians passage uses the images of adoption into God's love. Because Christ came to earth as a human, we are made legal children of God. We "are no longer a slave but a child, and if a child then also an heir" (Galatians 4:7). This is a great change: to go from slaves to children of the Lord.

In Luke's writing we read the story of Mary and Joseph taking Jesus to Jerusalem for the purification ritual. During this visit two Temple adherents recognized the divinity of the child and proclaimed that with his presence a great change was to come upon the world, and a new relationship was to be established between God and humanity.

With Jesus in the world things are going to change.

Story: CHANGING COLORS

A few years ago a common breakfast cereal was distributing color-changing spoons in its packages. When the spoon was at room temperature, it was one color; but when dipped into the colder milk in the cereal, it changed color. Of course, we kept our spoons because we knew we'd be able to use them in church someday; but if you didn't keep yours, you should be able to pick one up at a local toy store or novelty shop. The item does not need to be a spoon. Any article you may have that can change its appearance easily will work for this story. Have your item and a cup of cold water and a cup of hot water nearby.

You will need:
Item that
   changes color
Cup of hot
   water
Cup of cold
   water

When the children have gathered (and there is not likely to be many of them, compared to last week), ask them a bit about their Christmas celebrations, traveling, and gift giving/getting. Ask them if they think anything is different now that Christmas has come and gone.

In fact, we are not much different. We tend to stay pretty much the same from one year to the next. But the reason for celebrating Christmas means that things are very different. Because Jesus Christ was born in Bethlehem, things are very different in the world.

Show them your spoon.

It is a simple thing. We use spoons every day, and we don't expect them to change, but this one does. Look, just by dipping this spoon in this cup, it comes up a different color. And if I dip it in this other cup, it changes color again! (*Depending on the water the spoon has been in, it becomes a different color.*)

Explain that believing in Jesus Christ is like being put into a different cup of water. It changes us so that we look different to other people.

We should always remember that with Jesus in the world and in our hearts, things are much different.

Second Sunday After Christmas Day
(A, B, C)

Message

God's love is forever. How do we understand eternity and forever in the mind of a child?

Commentary

The lectionary for this Sunday is the same for all three years of the cycle. A story based on these readings is included in *Come as a Child, Book 1*, and you may wish to refer to it. The following is another option for this Sunday's story.

These passages focus around God's salvation history as sung in the hymn that opens John's Gospel. While the Jeremiah passage rejoices in God's restored blessings, it centers on the promise that they shall never languish again (verse 12). In Ephesians Paul tells that Jesus was destined from the beginning of time as the salvation of humanity and then we are in turn heirs to this eternal salvation. The Gospel of John makes it clear, "In the beginning was the Word" — right from the very start. Adults, although perhaps never comprehending the ideas of eternity and infinity, are at least used to hearing the words and can accept them in the sermon. The challenge

Jeremiah
31:7-14

Psalm
147:12-20

Ephesians
1:3-14

John
1:1-18

for a children's message along this line is to find an image that can represent such an abstract concept and yet be an image to which the young children can relate.

Keywords

Eternity

Rope

Story: HOW LONG?

Get a rope at least one hundred feet long and longer, if you have it. The longer, the better. Have the rope coiled up in a bag, but practice with your coiling to be certain the rope will come out of the bag easily and untangled.

Gather the children.

You will need:
Rope

I have a rope here in my bag today. I wonder if you could figure out how long my rope is. How much rope do you think I could fit in this bag? (*Start pulling out the rope, a very little bit at first.*) **How much more do you think might be here?** (*Pull out more and more rope until the children get the sense that this might be endless rope.*) **Actually, there is an end to this rope, but it might take us a long time to get to the end.**

I actually had a rope long enough that I could give the loose end to one of the children to hold while I took the bag and let out the rope as I walked to the back of the church, out the doors, down the stairs, across the auditorium, and back up the back stairs into the sanctuary.

Could you imagine any rope that didn't have an end? I don't think we could. It is hard to think of a rope that would have no end. In the same way it is hard for us to imagine that time goes on forever and ever, that it will never stop. But that is how God has made it — it never ends. And do you know what? God has been looking after time ever since it was made. Jesus Christ has been with God all that time and will be with God forever, until time ends.

The good news is that since Jesus and God love you; they will love you for all time, which never ends. You will always be loved by God no matter how long you live, and even after. That's a long time.

Season of Epiphany

First Sunday After the Epiphany

(Baptism of the Lord)

Message

Water is an essential element, not only in our lives and in nature, but also in our spiritual lives.

Commentary

All of today's readings focus on water. First there is the movement of the Sprit of God over the face of the waters in Genesis. It was there at the beginning, even before God created light. This is important. In the psalm, "The voice of the LORD is over the waters" (Psalm 29:3). The New Testament readings talk of baptism in water. John the Baptist started his ministry baptizing people in the Jordan River. Jesus came to him and was baptized, and the Holy Spirit was seen in the form of a dove. Baptism in water continued to be an important practice in the young church, as we read in Acts of the baptism of the people in Ephesus. Again baptism coincided with evidence of the Holy Spirit's presence.

Story: WATER EVERYWHERE

Show the children a globe of the earth or a map of the world.

By holding a globe in certain ways, sometimes all you can see is water. There is a tremendous amount of water on the earth. Even if we don't see it from where we live, water makes up the bulk of the earth's surface. Similarly, water makes up about eighty-five percent of your body weight. That means if you were to dry out your body, take out all the water, if you could, you would go from weighing one hundred pounds to less than twenty pounds. We have to drink a lot of water to keep ourselves alive, and even if you're not drinking a lot of glasses of water each day, you take in a lot through the food you eat.

Genesis
1:1-5

Psalm 29

Acts 19:1-7

Mark
1:4-11

Keywords
Baptism
Globe
Holy Spirit
Water

You will need:
Globe

23

In the Bible water is often shown as an important part not only of our lives, but also of our souls. Jesus was baptized in water, which is why we use water when we baptize people today. The water reminds us of the Holy Spirit. When we go swimming, we are surrounded by water. When you are baptized, you are surrounded by the Holy Spirit.

Second Sunday After the Epiphany

1 Samuel
3:1-20

Psalm
139:1-6,
13-18

1 Corinthians
6:12-20

John
1:43-51

Keywords
Call
Prayer
Telephone

Message

God calls us all to be servants of God's gospel. Sometimes we hear the call clearly. Sometimes we are not so sure.

Commentary

When God called the prophet Samuel, Samuel was asleep in the Lord's house. Samuel was understandably confused since the "word of the LORD was rare in those days" (1 Samuel 3:1). He had to hear the call three times before he figured out who it was, and then it was only because Eli told him what to do. How many times does the chance to do something for God come, and we fail to answer because we do not understand, or we are asleep, or we are afraid? Similarly, Jesus called Philip and Nathanael. Nathanael was at first skeptical because he thought it was unlikely that any good could come from Nazareth. But when they came close to Jesus, Jesus easily identified himself and proved himself. The psalm reading and the passage from First Corinthians deal with our identity as believers in God. God knows who we are; it is important for us, then, to know who we are. When we identify ourselves as God's people, we are open to doing what God calls us to do.

Story: GOD CALLING

Show the children a telephone.

How many of you are allowed to answer the telephone at home? What is the first thing you say when you answer the telephone? Hello. Then the next thing is to find out who is calling. You ask them unless you recognize their voice right away. Once you know who it is, you know what to say.

Often in our lives we get the feeling that God is calling us, but we aren't sure if it's God. It may be a feeling that we should help someone, or maybe we are wondering about sharing something. God often speaks to us, but not always in a voice like on the telephone, so we have to be ready to recognize God in whatever way God is talking. (*You can add that the only way for the telephone to work in our system is if it's connected to phone lines.*) The same is true of understanding God's talking. We have to be connected. We do that by prayer and study.

You will need:
Telephone

Third Sunday After the Epiphany

Message

God calls us all to be servants of God's gospel. Sometimes we hear the call clearly. Sometimes we are not so sure.

Commentary

Jonah was reluctant to take his prophecy of doom to the people of Nineveh. When he finally got to Nineveh and walked for a day and proclaimed God's message, the people responded immediately. It is peculiar that the evil city was faster at doing God's will than God's own prophet. Despite the prophet's tardiness it was because of the city's rapid repentance that God changed God's mind about the calamity that was to come upon it.

Paul's sentiments in 1 Corinthians 7 are that the present order of the world is being thrown over, and those who believe in the gospel of Christ must act as though imminent change will come upon them. The disciples James and John were an impetuous pair, but this attribute was in their favor when they "immediately" left their father, Zebedee, and followed Christ. They were quickly able to see the special nature of this man and knew that no time should be wasted before they did his bidding.

Jonah
3:1-5, 10

Psalm
62:5-12

1 Corinthians
7:29-31

Mark 1:14-20

Story: WHAT'S THE RUSH?

Keywords

Emergency

Helping

Hurry

Rush

You will need:
Models or
pictures of
emergency
vehicles

For this story have a large toy ambulance or fire truck to illustrate the message. Pictures of emergency vehicles would be appropriate too. We just think each child's time in church should include something more than a big person talking at them. Ask the children about what sort of things they see that are often in a hurry.

Have you ever seen an ambulance, fire truck, or police car whiz by with alarms and lights? The people driving in these vehicles have important things to do, and they have to do them right away or else someone may get hurt. Maybe sometimes at home you have seen your mom or dad rushing around because the alarm clock didn't go off and they are late and they have to hurry; or else they're going to be late and some bad things will happen if they are late.

We are reminded in the Bible that we have to do things to help others and that we shouldn't wait to do them. The longer we wait, the more hurt there will be. We can do things right away to help people, to share good things, to be kind to someone as soon as he or she needs it; because when we wait, he or she suffers more. Remember how fast the ambulance has to go to help people? We should be fast in helping people.

Fourth Sunday After the Epiphany

Deuteronomy
18:15-20

Psalm 111

1 Corinthians
8:1-13

Mark
1:21-28

Message

It can often be confusing about what is true and what is a lie told to get your attention. We are promised in the Bible that God will always provide someone or something to show us the way.

Commentary

In the middle of the passages about the law in Deuteronomy, the author has inserted a paragraph about prophets and false prophets. God promises there will be someone to prophesy, to tell the truth. Throughout Israel's history these prophets appeared.

Some were heeded, others ignored. We may assume that other prophets existed, but their words were false and were not recorded.

Paul explains in Corinthians that even though many people hold to pagan beliefs, practices, and worries, the truly liberated Christian is free. The truth sets us free. Jesus established himself as a speaker of truth at the synagogue in Capernaum: "They were astounded at his teaching, for he taught them as one having authority, and not as the scribes" (Mark 1:22). The people obviously doubted the preaching they had received from their scribes.

Keywords

Groundhog

Fable

Truth

Story: THE TRUTH ABOUT GROUNDHOGS

This Sunday falls around February 2, Groundhog Day in North America. This is an especially peculiar celebration set aside for those of us who live through a long winter and look for anything to promise that spring is returning. As the legend goes, on February 2 the groundhog, a large ground-dwelling rodent about the size of a household cat, emerges from its winter hibernation. If the groundhog can see its shadow (in other words, if the sun is shining), the groundhog predicts that spring will not arrive for another six weeks (March 22). If there is no shadow, the groundhog announces that spring has arrived. This may sound like a far-fetched idea for a winter celebration, but we know of at least two communities that have built huge festivals around the Groundhog Day Theme. Punxsutawney, Pennsylvania, was featured in a great movie called "Groundhog Day" starring Bill Murray, Andie MacDowell, and of course, the star rodent, Punxsutawney Phil. Wiarton, Ontario, boasts that its groundhog festival features the only albino groundhog in captivity: Wiarton Willy. We're not making this up. We will use this theme in today's story.

The best thing to have for this illustration would be a stuffed toy groundhog, but we know they are difficult to come by. You may have to settle for a good picture of one from an encyclopedia or off the Internet. Your talk to the children should go along these lines.

If you know anything about the life of groundhogs, you know how they hibernate for the winter. This means they go off to sleep and don't wake up again until it gets warm outside. Wouldn't it be nice if we could live life the same way? What are some other animals that you know do this? On February 2 we make a fun remembrance of this hibernation idea, and we call this Groundhog Day. If the groundhog sees his shadow that day, then that means the sun is shining

today, but there will still be six more weeks until spring. If there is no shadow, then spring is supposed to start right away. How many of you believe this?

It is a nice tradition, but it's not likely going to make any difference whether the sun shines or not. What will make the difference is the movement of big air streams from the Gulf of Mexico and the Arctic Ocean and the tilting of the earth so that our part of the world gets closer to the sun and stuff like that. It's stuff that none of us really understands, but the professionals who study this promise us that is the way it goes.

It's important that we know whom to trust and whom to believe when we hear different stories and different ideas about how things work. Sometimes we are told cute stories, but in actual fact they are not true. The Bible promises us that there will always be someone to tell us the truth about God. That person is Jesus Christ, and we read about him in the Bible. Remember, when different people tell you different things about God, we can always get the true story from our Bible.

You will need:
Model or picture of a groundhog

Fifth Sunday After the Epiphany

Isaiah 40:21-31

Psalm 147:1-11, 20c

1 Corinthians 9:16-23

Mark 1:29-39

Message

God's message must go out to the people. You need to go where they are; meet them in their place. Let the gospel fill them.

Commentary

Paul tells us that he became all things to all people, in the hopes of bringing them the message of the gospel. Was he being underhanded? No, on the contrary, he was showing us the fullness of the gospel, that it has meaning for all people in all circumstances. Contrary to early missionary practices, preaching the gospel does not mean exporting your own culture. The gospel has applications in every culture; it must be malleable and adaptable. While at the beginning of the Mark passage, we read of people coming to Jesus, Jesus told Simon, Andrew, James, and John that he wanted to go out to the towns to preach. He wanted to go where people are. The psalmist says it a little differently; God does not delight in things that this world places importance on (things culturally based), but in those who are filled up with love for God.

Story: ONE CUP FILLS ALL

Hold a glass pitcher of water up and show everyone the beauty of it, crystal clear and pure. Ask the children to describe the water to you. Draw out as many adjectives as you can. Should anyone mention its shape, pause and direct everyone's attention to the shape. Chances are that no one will, because they are used to seeing water in so many forms. That's what makes this an excellent object lesson. Ask the children to describe the shape of the water in your pitcher. Now pull out the first bottle and pour water into it: "See, it now has a different shape." Continue to fill each bottle, each time commenting on the shape the water has assumed. Now draw attention to the people in the congregation.

Look around you. God made people of many different ent shapes and sizes. Each person is loved by God. God pours out love into all of us, regardless of the length of our hair, the shape of our bodies, or the life that we've lived. God's love is like water and fills each one of us.

Keywords
Evangelism
Shapes
Water

You will need:
Several pitchers of water (one might be enough)

Several bottles of interesting shapes

Sixth Sunday After the Epiphany

Message

God loves us. God hears our cries of pain and lovingly heals us.

Commentary

These four texts tell us of God's healing powers. The Second Kings passage and the Mark passage deal with physical healing, the healing of lepers. The psalm and First Corinthians passages deal with God's redemptive power in the emotional, the spiritual, and the imperishable dimensions of our lives. This is a tricky concept to communicate to adults, let alone children. Perhaps this

2 Kings
5:1-14

Psalm 30

1 Corinthians
9:24-27

Mark
1:40-45

is why this theme is hammered away at by so many biblical writers, because every generation needs to learn for the first time that God loves us. Just as soon as we learn, we forget and need to be reminded that God continues to love us. Not only does God love us, but God also hears our cries of pain, and God does heal us both physically and spiritually, inwardly and outwardly.

Story: VALENTINE'S DAY

(This Sunday usually falls near St. Valentine's Day.)

Does everyone know what is special about February 14? Yes, it is St. Valentine's Day. St. Valentine lived a long time ago. He served God at a time when this could get you into trouble. There were many people who did not like hearing about God's love; and so they tried to shut people up who taught about God's love, and who followed Jesus, by putting them in jail and often killing them. That's what happened to St. Valentine. He was arrested and put in jail for telling people about God's love. St. Valentine knew he was going to be killed, and so he wrote notes to his friends, telling them to be courageous and to keep following Jesus no matter what.

He told them to keep telling people about God's love. St. Valentine didn't want to be forgotten, and he didn't want people to forget that for him, telling people that God loves them was more important than his own life. So he signed his notes, "Remember your Valentine" and "I love you."

The people who killed St. Valentine celebrated a festival of love on February 15 (Lupercalia), and we think that February 14 is the day that St. Valentine was killed. So St. Valentine's friends and followers thought that a marvelous way to remember their Valentine was to celebrate God's love for each of us and our love for one another on February 14. And so every year they passed notes telling one another that they loved them, and to "Remember your Valentine." And that is how Valentine's Day began. It will always be mixed up with thoughts about romantic love and things like that, that moms and dads will worry about, but they're missing the whole point, aren't they? Valentine's Day is the day to remind everyone you know about God's love for him or her and your love for him or her.

And so I have a valentine for each of you, because God loves each of you, and I want you to know that; and because I love each of you, and I want you to know that; and because telling you that is more important than my own life.

You will need:
Valentine cards (one for each child, or make one for everyone in the church)

Keywords

Love
Valentine

Message

Forgiveness is a hard thing to give. Aren't we glad God is a lot freer with it than we are?

Isaiah
43:18-25

Psalm 41

2 Corinthians
1:18-22

Mark 2:1-12

Commentary

What is easier, to forgive sins or to heal someone with a disability? When Jesus posed this question to the scribes, he was not equating the two, but rather making a point. We often find it easier to believe in miracles of healing than miracles of forgiveness. The physical trauma, we can carry around on a pallet like someone who cannot walk, but transgressions against us, the sins of others, we carry closer and longer and cannot give them up. Isaiah tells us that God's forgiveness blots out our sins, and God does not remember them. Why can't we do the same? Jesus used the man who could not walk as a living parable — the people believed that Jesus healed him, and they were awestruck by the act; but they would not accept that Jesus could forgive the man his sins.

Story: FORGIVE AND FORGET

For this story you will need an example of a time when you were hurt physically. Any scars you have that you can show the children are helpful. You may have the cast, splint, or crutches that you used. Bring them and use them as visual aids. Maybe even one of the children was recently hurt — let him or her be the visual aid. Use your own scars and stories, of course. (We all have them!) We used Jim's six-inch scar on his leg as an example.

You will need:
Medical prop (crutches, cast, or splint)

I was hurt once really bad when I was fifteen years old. I went camping with my family, my cousin Ralph, and my Uncle Henry. My Uncle Henry was a carpenter; he worked on some of the big ships that sail the Great Lakes. Uncle Henry brought one of his saws camping. It was about three feet long and very sharp. Uncle Henry always hung his saw up on a tree so no one would get hurt. One evening after supper Ralph and I were using Uncle Henry's saw to cut up

Keywords

Forgiveness
Healing
Injury

some wood for a campfire. When we were finished, I laid the saw against a tree; I didn't hang it up like I had been shown. Later that night when I got up to go to the washroom, I was walking across the campsite, and I walked right into the saw. It cut into my leg as clean as a surgeon's knife. I knew I had hurt myself bad, but I didn't want to wake everyone up, so I limped to the washroom and looked at the cut in the light. It wasn't bleeding, but I thought I should wash it out. I turned on the water, and as soon as the water touched the cut, blood came gushing out. I wrapped it in a towel and hurried as best as I could back to the campsite. A few minutes later I was sandwiched between my dad and my Uncle Henry as they drove me through the North Ontario night to the Kapuskasing hospital a half hour away.

Now if you look at the scar, it has healed completely. The doctor stitched up the muscle and the skin, and I rested it for a couple of weeks. Now it's as good as new. You see, physical injuries that you can see are things easy to heal. God healed me by providing the wonderful doctor and the hospital and my dad and Uncle Henry to get me there.

But sometimes I do things that are worse than leaving a saw on the ground: I might say something that hurts someone's feelings. I may do something unkind or not do something I should. And then I hurt really badly inside. Sometimes I feel just awful. But when I pray to God and ask God to forgive me, God does, and God heals me inside. When I look at this scar, it reminds me that God heals me, inside and out. And just as God forgives me for my sins, I want to forgive the people around me who hurt me. I'm trying to learn to love people the way that God loves me.

Eighth Sunday After the Epiphany

Message

A new relationship requires new ways of being.

Commentary

Poor Hosea. He longed to create a new relationship with an unfaithful wife. He longed for the relationship they had in their youth. But these things cannot be reclaimed. If you have ever counseled a couple where one of them has been unfaithful, you know that the old relationship can never be again. This reality did not prevent Hosea from crying out for renewed relationship. How many times have we been unfaithful to God? And yet God, as Hosea preached, is open to rebuilding the relationship again and again. As the psalmist tells us, God forgives all our iniquity and renews our youth. So was Hosea wrong? Can we reclaim the relationship from our youth? No. With the help of God, we build a new one each time. It's not the same as the old one. It's different, and it can be better. Jesus tells us in Mark that the new relationship requires new ways of being, new ways of under-standing, and new ways of acting towards the people around us.

Story: NAME THAT TUNE

Here's a story that will really date you and your audience. It will even date this book as CDs become a thing of the past, but hey, you'll adapt.

Everyone loves music. Music defines our lives; it marks the passage of time. We grownups listen to music that was different than our parents' music. They listened to different music than their parents, and on and on. The music you listen to is different than what your parents listen to. Different does not mean better or worse; it just means different. For instance, when I was young, we used to listen to: (*Insert some favorite lyrics from a song from your youth; try and pick one that sounds particularly corny or humorous.*) On the other hand, you listen to much more serious songs like: (*Again, find some really goofy lyrics, but don't degrade the music; prejudice ruins this whole story.*) Not only has the style of music changed, but the way in which it is carried has changed too.

(*Show the children a vinyl album.*) This is a vinyl album. It holds about forty-five minutes of music that's been etched into the surface of the record. It was pretty amazing in its day. Not only did it carry music, but the cover was a great place for artworks and big pictures of your favorite group or singer. Then came the eight-track tape deck. You don't find these anymore except in old pickup trucks and yard sales.

Hosea
2:14-20

Psalm
103:1-13, 22

2 Corinthians
3:1-6

Mark
2:13-22

Keywords
Cassette
Compact disc
Eight track
Music
New
Records
Relationships

You will need:
Vinyl album
record player
and vinyl
album (a
45-rpm)

Eight-track
tape player
and eight-
track tape

Cassette
player and
cassette

CD player
and CD

(*Show the children a cassette.*) **This is a cassette. You still see these, and people still buy them and play them. They hold a lot of music, but in the sun, the tape inside can melt; and in the cold, the tape can get brittle and break. The music is stored magnetically on the cassette. You can erase the whole cassette by placing a magnet on it.**

(*Show the children a compact disc.*) **This is a compact disc. We usually call it a CD. It holds a lot of music, it's small (that's what they mean by "compact"), and it's pretty durable. The music is burned into the disc using a laser beam. And if you would like to hear the difference, listen:**

Play an album on the record player (or tape a record onto a cassette and play the cassette). Try to get one with lots of hisses and pops! Play the CD. Go for clarity; pick a CD that has lots of instruments, crisp highs, and deep bass.

Now we could record this album onto the CD, and we would hear all the same pops and hisses — they would not change. In fact, the CD would make those imperfections crisp and clear, forever.

God doesn't want us to be imperfect forever. God wants us to learn a new song and carry it in a new way. Jesus wanted people to see a new way to follow God and a new way to live that was different from the old ways. Jesus wanted the people he talked with to have a new relationship with God, and a new relationship means that they should think and act differently than they used to.

Ninth Sunday After the Epiphany

Message

Celebrate the Lord's Day.

Commentary

Both Old Testament texts tie worship on the sabbath to God's act of salvation in hearing the cries of the Israelites and bringing them out of Egypt. This act was so great that it requires not a moment in time when we reflect on its occurrence, but one day in every seven when we pause, give thanks, and marvel at God's wonderful work. Deuteronomy echoes the Genesis account of creation: "Six days you shall labor and do all your work. But the seventh day is a sabbath to the LORD your God" (verses 13-14). That is, God created the world in six days and rested on the seventh. Even God took a day to marvel at God's own creative Spirit.

The first question to ask is, did God need to rest because of physical exhaustion? The answer is an unequivocal no. The works of God are so wonderful, even God pauses to consider their beauty. Observing the seventh day as a day of rest is not for physical regeneration. It is to ensure that there is a day where no business (read that as busy-ness) impedes us from remembering what God has done, whether in Creation, in the history of Israel, or in our own lives, and then honoring God appropriately. This day was given to us as a day to focus on the goodness and greatness of God.

Jesus' statement recorded in Mark that "the sabbath was made for humankind" (verse 27) has been used to justify a day of doing nothing, often not even worshiping God. But what Jesus implied was that the sabbath was made for people to honor God, not to honor the sabbath itself. The sabbath is a sign that points to something greater. It means more than just a day of rest.

Deuteronomy
5:12-15

Psalm
81:1-10

2 Corinthians
4:5-12

Mark
2:23–3:6

Story: SIGNS, SIGNS, EVERYWHERE A SIGN

You will need: Signs (make your own, or download some from a web site)

How many of you kids have your driver's license? Not many, I guess. However, I will bet that even though you don't drive a car, you know an awful lot about safety on the road, and what the rules of the road are. Let's take a little test. I'm going to show you a sign, and I want you to tell me what it means. Ready? Here we go. (*Hold up the signs you have, such as stop, walk, slippery road, railroad crossing, deer crossing, or steep hill. Let the children yell out their answers. If they get stuck, allow the parents to help.*) **You did pretty good. Now let's see if you know some different signs. Ready? Here we go.** (*The next set of signs can include whatever you'd like to use, such as a peace sign, a heart, a cross, and so forth. The last sign is one that simply says "Sunday." They will read it; ask them what it means, then proceed.*)

Sunday is a sign just like any of these other signs. Sunday means to rest, to worship, and to honor God. The Bible tells us that we should honor God by treating Sunday differently from all of the other days. When we treat Sunday as a special day, it becomes a sign to us that we recognize all of the things God has done for us, all of the creation that is ours to explore, and all of the miracles God works in our lives. Sunday is a sign to us; it reminds us that God takes care of us. When you look at the calendar and you see the word *Sunday* getting closer, it's a sign to you to slow down and to get ready to remember all of the things that God has done for you.

Last Sunday After the Epiphany
(Transfiguration Sunday)

2 Kings
2:1-12

Psalm
50:1-6

2 Corinthians
4:3-6

Mark 9:2-9

Message

Let God's light shine in you and light up the whole world.

Commentary

When Elijah was taken up in a whirlwind, Elisha was left with his predecessor's cloak. He took this mantle and crossed the Jordan in the same fashion as Elijah and he had crossed it moments before, by parting the waters. Then Elisha went on to do many great miracles, many more than Elijah himself had done. Elijah's light continued to shine, and shone even brighter, in his disciple Elisha.

In the Gospel of Mark we read of the blinding light on the mountain at the Transfiguration. We know that Jesus' light continued to shine in the lives and work of his disciples. In fact, when you think about it, Jesus' ministry was an incredibly short period of time. Jesus changed the world more in three years than anyone else had done before or since. Nevertheless, his disciples carried his mantle and continued his ministry, multiplying the number of people who heard the good news of God's salvation.

We must not forget that it is God who causes this light to shine in us. Elijah made it clear to Elisha that it was not a given that he would inherit Elijah's spirit; that was God's choice.

Paul put it plainly: It is God who brought light into the darkness by sheer will alone. It is God who causes the light to shine in us, and it is that light that shines in us that we must let shine through us into the world.

Keywords
Candle
Light
Transfiguration

Story: THIS LITTLE LIGHT OF MINE

You will need:
Vigil candles
Matches
Large central candle

In preparation for this story someone should be prepared to turn off all the lights in the church. The vigil candles should be handed out prior to the story so that everyone in the congregation has one. Invite the children to sit so that they are facing the congregation. Speak to them along these lines:

There are many ways of talking about God and God's spirit. One way that the writers of the Bible used to talk about God's spirit was light. Now, we all know that light is important, and we know that light always overcomes dark; dark can never overcome light. Light makes darkness shrink and flee, and light can keep growing and growing. (*Light the large central candle.*)

The light of God's spirit shines so that everyone can see it. Even the people in the back of the church can see the flame. (*Take two vigil candles and light them.*) God's light shines in the hearts of everyone who believes. Once God's light is shining in you, you can be the light for the person who lives beside you.

Begin lighting the congregation's candles; you may want to send someone down the aisle lighting the candles of each row. Take a moment to allow the entire congregation to have their candles lit.

Look at the sea of lights that all began with this one candle. That's just how God's spirit spreads throughout the whole world, from one believer to another, and so on, and so on, and so on!

Season of Lent

Genesis
9:8-17

Psalm
25:1-10

1 Peter
3:18-22

Mark
1:9-15

Keywords
Baptism
Grace
Rain
Water

Message

The grace of God is offered to us as free as rain from the sky. Does it fall on us and produce abundance, or do we let it run off our raincoats and umbrellas to be soaked up by the ground?

Commentary

After the flood in Genesis God made a promise with Noah that never again would a flood destroy the earth (verse 11). The rainbow, which we know today is caused by light shining through water, was a sign of that covenant. A covenant is a promise between two parties to stick to their sides in any agreement. The human side in this agreement was to keep God's commandments, although oddly enough there is no mention of this at this point in the story. This covenant with Noah only mentions the things that God will do, with no specific mention of what will be expected of the humans for their part.

Psalm 25 reflects this covenant in verse 10 with the assurance that things go well for those who keep the Lord's decrees. The psalm also recognizes, however, that we are poor at keeping this up and appeals to God to "not remember the sins of my youth or my transgressions; according to your steadfast love" (verse 7).

The writer of First Peter makes a connection between the story of Noah and the baptism of Christ. Both are a passage through water to a state of grace and acceptance by God.

Mark's version of the baptism of Christ is short and omits the dialogue between Jesus and John that Matthew plays up. There doesn't seem to be much need for Mark to make a big deal out of it. It just happened, and the voice from heaven spoke, and now let's get on with the rest of the story.

The baptismal image of water for the spirit of God is central to all our Christian faith traditions. In most areas of the world water comes to us from the skies, free for the taking. So does God's grace.

Story: LET'S MAKE A LITTLE RAIN

In this story time we'd like to work on this image that God's grace rains down upon us. There are all sorts of ways to represent rain to the children, and we hope your imagination and your courage will be the guiding principle this time. Use any or many of the following suggestions to show the effects of rain upon us. A bowl of water is easy to arrange. Dip your fingers in the bowl and flick the water around, on yourself, or on the gathered children, if you dare. A spray bottle is a good tool, if you can adjust the output from streaming to gentle mist. Some children may find it pleasant, but others may be upset to get a few drops of water on them, so use your best judgment as to what to do with these items. Rain sticks are becoming a common sound instrument. They are available at many music stores or at developing country craft outlet stores. When tipped from end to end, hundreds of tiny pellets inside tumble through the tube, creating a sound very much like rain.

After you have done some things to get the children thinking about rain, get them to talk about it.

Where does it come from? Where does it go? Why is it important?

Explain that the stories we read in the Bible today are all about water and rain and how God used them to show God's love to God's people.

Just as rain refreshes the ground and makes life good for us, so God refreshes us and makes life good for us.

> **You will need:**
> Items to help the children think about rain

Genesis
17:1-7,
15-16

Psalm
22:23-31

Romans
4:13-25

Mark
8:31-38

Keywords

Blindfolds
Faith
Trust
Trust fall

Message

Trust and faith in God's promises are part of the covenant. Can we learn to trust God by following the examples of the people in the Bible?

Commentary

Just like last week's Old Testament reading, this week's reading offers us an account of God making a covenant with God's chosen people. The covenant with Noah came with a rainbow as a sign. With Abram and Sarai it came with a change of name so they would remember this covenant, which was to be as much a part of their lives as their names. Unlike the covenant with Noah, the one with Abraham and Sarah did have a human condition laid upon it; but this part is omitted in the lectionary selection. Decide if you should insert the missing verses 8 to 14. The important human element of this covenant, regardless of the missing verses, is that it depends upon a strong trust that Abraham and Sarah (and all their descendants, including us) must place upon God's promises. Consider how difficult it must have been for Abraham and Sarah to believe that at their advanced age they would bear a son and become the ancestors of huge nations. This same trust and faith is what Paul stresses in the Romans verses.

The Gospel story for this day tells of how Peter showed little faith or trust in Christ's words and was rebuked for it — rebuked to the point of being likened to Satan! In the charge to the disciples that followed this, Jesus explained that God is actually ashamed for those of us who do not put our trust in God.

Psalm 22 starts as a lament, but by the time we get to the passage we read as part of the lectionary, the writer has come around to thanksgiving and joy. A transition like this is possible when we learn to trust in the Lord: "God did not hide God's face from me, but heard when I cried to God" (verse 24, adapted).

Story: DO YOU TRUST ME?

Many simple exercises and games teach us trust and dependence upon other people. Trust and dependence upon

God come more from personal experience, but we can show examples of that trust by doing some simple games.

The "trust fall" offers a visual example of placing our trust in someone else. Have someone volunteer to stand about three feet in front of you, facing away from you. Tell the volunteer to close his or her eyes and remain rigid and straight as a board. Have the person fall back into your waiting arms. The volunteer cannot see you, so he or she will have to trust that you will be there to prevent him or her from hitting the ground. You may find it difficult to get a volunteer for this, but then you can point out that if it is so hard for us to trust someone in such a simple game, how much harder must it be for us to trust God when we are asked to do difficult things like Abraham and Sarah were asked?

Another easier trust game involves putting a blindfold on one person and then leading that person around the room and through the crowds of people. Not only does the blindfolded person have to trust the guide, but he or she must also trust that no one in the crowd would deliberately try to trip or play a trick on him or her.

In our Christian lives we are always expected to place our trust in God. We have many good examples in the Bible of people trusting God. Let us hope we can be as trusting in our faith as these people were.

Third Sunday in Lent

Message

Many things in life require us to take a good second look before we know the truth. This happens in the Bible too.

Exodus 20:1-17

Psalm 19

Commentary

The Old Testament reading today gives another account of a covenant made between God and God's people. The Ten Commandments are pivotal to our faith, and perhaps a young person has the impression that Christian faith is all about following rules. We know a lot of adults do. With our human tendency to avoid restrictive rules and our desire to live free from restraint, it is

1 Corinthians 1:18-25

John 2:13-22

Keywords

Anger

Optical
  illusion

Rules

natural to express aversion to commandments. But these rules are not just rules for the sake of keeping control over us. They are created to express the love of God for creation, just like a parent puts limits on what a child is allowed to do out of love, not power.

The beautiful Psalm 19 expresses joy and fulfillment in knowing and following the law of the Lord. It is not restrictive, but rather more desired than gold and sweeter than honey.

The passage in First Corinthians mentions that at first look, the cross is a ridiculous image for the God of the cosmos. How could God, according to human wisdom, end up crucified? But with a second look from those of us who love God, we see the image of death on the cross as the power of God, not the weakness of God.

The story of Jesus' anger in clearing the Temple is a difficult one to address for children. Anger is a strong emotion for any age, and it should be approached carefully. We should not, however, dismiss this very real emotion; and we must not avoid this story, as it is a real and vibrant account in the life of Jesus. We approach this incident as another event where things may not be what they seem. Just because Jesus was angry did not mean he did not love the people in the story. Just as when our parents may be angry at us sometimes, it does not mean they have stopped loving us. As a matter of fact, when they are angry, it may show their love, because the cause of their anger may be something we have done to put ourselves into danger.

Story: THINGS ARE NOT AS THEY SEEM

As a visual support to this approach, we need to show things that are different than they appear; and we need to stress to the children they must look deeper and closer at situations, even Bible stories, to understand them. We used a picture postcard that shows a flatbed truck with one potato taking up the entire load. The caption reads, "This is how we grow 'em in PEI." When you look closely, you can tell the truck is a toy miniature, while the potato is a regular kitchen size. It gives the illusion of one huge potato.

You can probably check novelty shops for other pictures or items that depend upon our tendency to give things only a quick glance. The whole magic industry depends upon us only seeing certain things and not seeing the whole picture. We made use of optical illusions in a story in Book 1 (see Come as a Child, Book 1, *page 29). There are also many good web sites with examples of optical illusions that you can download and print out to make the point that things are not as they seem.*

After making the point that things are not as they seem, tell the children that many times in Bible stories it is important for us to look deeper than what we see in our first reading. When we give good thought to the Ten Commandments, we learn that they are very good for us and are not restrictive. When we carefully consider a story of Jesus showing his anger, we may learn that the anger was an example of Christ's love and not hatred for those people.

You will need:
An optical illusion

Fourth Sunday in Lent

Message

We know God loves us even when we don't deserve it.

Commentary

It never ceases to amaze us how God put up with the wandering Israelites. Around every corner they seemed to have some gripe or some transgression to bring before the Lord, who miraculously brought them out of bondage in the first place, delivered them through the parted waters of the Red Sea, fed them, and protected them. They seemed to like to complain, but don't be too down on them for this until you have taken a good long look at your own attitude toward God's blessings in your life. Here again, in the story in Numbers, is an account of complaints brought to Moses and God. They sound so much like children complaining they don't like the food. Although God was the agent of their punishment in this story, God also provided the cure for these belligerent people. God's forgiveness always seems to be able to come to the fore.

The psalmist remembers the sinful ways of the ancestors and that they suffered for it. The psalmist also notes, however, that God's "steadfast love endures forever" (Psalm 107:1). Have you ever noticed that there is no passage that says God's punishment or anger lasts forever? But there are many places where we are told that God's love lasts forever.

Numbers 21:4-9

Psalm 107:1-3, 17-22

Ephesians 2:1-10

John 3:14-21

Keywords
Forgiveness
Love

In Ephesians we are reminded that God has brought us back to life from the sins that held us. God is rich in mercy, and God's great love has made it possible for God to keep us as God's children, despite our disobedient ways. John 3:16 is indeed the most quoted of Bible passages, and not much has to be said about it here. It just simply reminds us that God is love.

Story: HOW DO YOU KNOW SOMEONE LOVES YOU?

Ask the children about how they know certain things are about to happen.

How do you know it's going to snow soon? How do you know it's time to go to bed? How do you know you're getting bigger?

The final question should be, "How do you know someone loves you?" They may give answers like, "They care for you," "They give you gifts," and "They send you letters and cards." Work their answers around until you can get the most important sign of all: "They forgive you for doing something bad." This is a concept that younger children will not know how to verbalize, so don't wait a long time for them to come up with it. One way to bring it out is to ask if any of them remember doing something wrong — something that upset their parents or their teacher. The children may be unwilling to admit it in public. Don't force them, but ask them to think about the situation in mind. After they have done something wrong, their parents or teachers may punish them so that they know not to do it again. After the punishment, and often even without any punishment, their parents go on loving them. This is just like it is in the Bible.

In this way we know that God loves us, because God has forgiven us for the bad things we did. We know this because of one of the most popular verses in the Bible: "For God so loved the world that he gave his only son . . ."

It would be a good visual enhancement to have this verse written out large on a big sheet or on a poster.

Message

Jesus died, but was raised to life again. This is a hard idea for children, but perhaps by using an example of something familiar, it may bring some understanding.

Commentary

It was probably no easier for the disciples to understand Jesus' prediction about death and resurrection than it is for us today, or for our children. Jesus tried many times to explain it to them, and the Gospel reading today is one more attempt on his part. Jesus left a very good children's story example, however, when he compared it to a grain of wheat that must fall to the ground and die to bring forth new life. Unless the grain does this, it never produces new grain.

The Hebrews passage reminds us that Jesus did not give in to temptation to avoid suffering. Jesus did suffer, but because of that he was made perfect. (Don't you bring Melchizedek into the children's story!) Jeremiah's prophecy declares that God will make a new covenant. The covenant includes God's promise: "I will forgive their iniquity, and remember their sin no more" (Jeremiah 31:34).

Story: WANTED — DEAD OR ALIVE

Around this time of year you should have no trouble finding a potted bulb that is in flower. Along with this have a collection of bulbs, some of which have the beginnings of new shoots showing through. If you don't have these in your garage, a local nursery will be glad to unload some on you for this purpose.

Do you know of anything that is dead and alive at the same time? Do you know of anything that dies first and then is alive? Most things we think of are alive first and then they die. But take a look at these things I have here. (*Show the bulbs to the children.*) **They are all dry and brown, and they look pretty dead, don't they? As a matter of fact, they were very colorful flowers last summer, but then in the fall they died off and dried up and look like they do now — dead.**

Jeremiah
31:31-34

Psalm
51:1-12

Hebrews
5:5-10

John
12:20-33

Keywords
Bulbs
Dormancy
Flowers
Resurrection

But now look at these other bulbs. (*Show the bulbs with new shoots.*) These have a shoot coming out of them. This shoot is a new plant that will grow into a beautiful flower in a few weeks. They will look something like this with all the leaves and color. (*Show the potted flowers.*)

Before it reaches that stage, the plants have to go through a whole winter of looking dead and dried up. This is often the way in nature. We plant things and they seem to die in the ground, but then after a short time they spring up into something new and fresh. Jesus said that a grain of wheat had to die in order to bring life to a new wheat plant. When he said this, he meant that he himself would die, but then from his death would come new life for all of those who love him. He was willing for that to happen to show the world they could not kill God's love. He lost his human life, but he was the real winner. We are the people who follow his way. We are the new life that has grown from his sacrifice. I want you to remember that Jesus died so that we could really live. To help you remember, I want each of you to take one of these things and plant them and see new life come from these "dead" things.

Give a bulb or two to each of the children to take home and plant. Most bulbs require a winter underground to "harden off," but there may be time left in your area for this to happen. An alternative is for you to have read this story a few months in advance. In that case you could force bulbs into readiness by putting them in the refrigerator for six to eight weeks prior to doing this story. But what are the chances of you being that organized?

Sixth Sunday in Lent

(Passion Sunday or Palm Sunday)

Message

There are several stories and legends involving natural objects that show the story of Jesus. Here is another one.

Commentary

The Passion story of Christ is hard to understand for many people. The positive images of Christmas that every child knows are replaced by the sad, solemn images of death and suffering. These are not images we often share with young people. In Isaiah we read a passage of a suffering person who willingly gave up his life and therefore was assured he would not be ashamed. The Philippians hymn is another version of what the Passion story meant to that community. The Gospel reading includes the whole of the Passion story, starting with the anointing in Bethany and ending with burial in the tomb. If the whole story is read in church, this illustration of the sand dollar may provide a welcome break.

Story: LEGEND OF THE SAND DOLLAR

A sand dollar is an interesting mollusk in roughly a circular shape, but with five radiating segments. These can be purchased at nature stores. We have seen them at pet stores, where they are sold as decorations for aquariums. When getting natural objects verify with the vendor that they have not been collected from any nature protection areas or that the particular item you are getting is not an endangered or threatened species. If you cannot get a real one, then a good-sized picture will do.

Show a sand dollar to your children and tell the story of the sand dollar.

The sand dollar is one of the most unusual specimens of marine life. They are often used as decorations at Christmas and Easter because people see in their markings symbols that remind them of the birth, crucifixion, and resurrection of Christ. Some see in the outline on the front of the shell a five-pointed star that represents the star of Bethlehem; others see this outline as an Easter lily. The five narrow, elliptical openings symbolize the five wounds made in the body of Christ during crucifixion. When you turn the shell over, you will see the outline of a poinsettia—the most popular Christmas flower. If you break the shell open, five objects will fall out that represent either the angels who sang to the shepherds, or doves, the most recognized symbol of peace.

Isaiah
50:4-9a

Psalm
31:9-16

Philippians
2:5-11

Mark
14:1–15:47

Keywords
Christmas
Crucifixion
Passion
Sand dollar

You will need:
Sand dollar

Season of Easter

Isaiah
25:6-9

Psalm
118:1-2,
14-24

1 Corinthians
15:1-11

Mark 16:1-8

Keywords
Batteries
Light
New life
Resurrection

Message

In the resurrection of Jesus Christ, God has shown God's power over death. This power is applied to God's children.

Commentary

Isaiah professed of a future salvation promised to God's people. This blessed state of affairs is compared to a great feast with the best of wine and foods. As well as a great party, God is promising to do away with all the things that bring us down, all the things that sadden us. The most impressive part, though, seems to be the idea of abolishing death itself. Only God can overcome death.

The psalmist rejoices that he or she has not been left to die, but has triumphed because of the strength of the Lord: "This is the day that the LORD has made" (Psalm 118:24). Paul, although never meeting Christ before the crucifixion, is able to relate to us what had been passed on to him from others. But the true power of his vision of Christ came from his encounter on the Damascus road as described in Acts 9.

The Mark account of the resurrection is perhaps the simplest of the four Gospels, but it says everything that has to be said. Christ has been raised from the dead. He is not in the tomb. Death cannot contain the glory of God.

Story: POWER TO SEE

Have a flashlight with dead batteries inside. Have some fresh replacement batteries handy.

Today we celebrate the resurrection of Jesus Christ. He was killed. He was dead. They put him in a grave and believed his life was over. But when they went to visit that grave later, they found that the body was not there. Instead, there was a young man dressed in a white robe who told them that Jesus had been raised from the dead. To be raised from the dead is a fantastic and incredible thing.

Show the children a flashlight that seems to have been dead for some time. When you turn on the switch, no light comes from it. But this flashlight can be given new life and new light simply by replacing the batteries that give it life. Put in the new batteries and shine the light around for the children to see.

As we are able to give this light new life by simply replacing the batteries, so God is able to give us new life by simply filling our spirits with God's love.

You will need:
Flashlight
Batteries

Second Sunday of Easter

Message

We can do much more when we are in unity than when we are apart.

Acts
4:32-35

Psalm 133

1 John
1:1–2:2

John
20:19-31

Commentary

Psalm 133 praises the life of faithful unity. It is a short psalm, and the message is clear: living in unity is a blessed thing.

The early disciples certainly saw the need to stick together "for fear." It was not a pleasant time for them right after the crucifixion and resurrection. They were afraid and confused; but by staying together, they were able to console and uplift one another. Into this fearful gathering Christ made his appearance and assured the followers that this was not the end. In Acts we read of how the early apostles held together and shared their possessions. Here again, the benefits of working and living and sharing together are made obvious by the fact that from this fledgling group grew the worldwide church that we have now.

Story: STICK TOGETHER

Have a collection of sticks with you for this story. They should be about two feet long and no thicker than your fingers.

You will need:
Two sticks
per child,
about two
feet long and
as thick as
your fingers

String

Speak to the children along these lines:

I want you to take a look around you. You may see your own parents, brothers, sisters, aunts, uncles, cousins, and friends. All of the people gathered here are a part of our congregation. We come together each week because we all want to worship God in the same way. We believe the same things about God and about how God wants us to live. We all care about one another. Everyone here is your brother and sister. Everyone who is older than you will look out for you and care for you. Everyone who is younger than you will depend on you to look out for him or her.

I brought each of you two sticks. (*Pass them out.*) Now I want you to take one of the sticks and break it. (*Break one yourself.*) That was pretty easy, wasn't it? To break one stick is pretty easy. Now I want you to pick up the other stick and pass it back to me. Now I have one stick from each of you. I'm going to bind them together with this string. These sticks are now tied together the same way that you are tied to everyone else here. What happens when I try to break them this time? I can't. Together they are stronger than they were individually.

The pressure on one stick is shared by all the others, those above, beneath, and on each side. In the same way you are protected and supported by the people in this church. We are all tied together by the love we share for God. That is the string that ties us together. Whatever pressures you feel throughout your life that threaten to break you like a twig, the people in this church will support you, protect you, and bear the strain for you. That's what it means to be the church.

Third Sunday of Easter

Message

God does not necessarily give us what we want. God gives us what we need.

Commentary

We do not always know what is best for us. The man at the gates who confronted Peter and John was seeking money to stay alive. Having abandoned all hope of walking or working, he was carried by his friends to a prime begging location, and here he asked for handouts from worshipers as they entered the Temple. Peter told him he had no gold or silver, but Peter offered him something more, something the man never even asked for. He was healed.

In Luke, Jesus appeared before the disciples, showed them his wounds, ate some fish, and opened their eyes to the Scriptures. We know they had questions in their hearts, but we can only assume what their questions were. What was it that they were wanting from Jesus? Were they looking for assurance that they would be safe, that what happened to him would not happen to them? Was the overthrow of the Romans now at hand with Jesus back among them? Whatever their questions were, Jesus gave them something they had not asked for: Jesus opened their eyes and gave them understanding. In fact, he made them witnesses to God's greatness; for some of them, that sealed their fate to a martyr's death.

Story: WHAT DO YOU WANT?

Do you know the difference between wanting something and needing something? Your parents have trouble with these words. Dad says he *needs* **a new stereo; Mom says no, he** *wants* **a new stereo.** (*We won't suggest any other variations lest we create offense gender-wise. Make up your own variations based on your congregation's demographics.*) **Water is something that we sometimes need, and something that we sometimes want. Let's take a little test:**

If you're a little thirsty before you go to bed, do you NEED water, or do you WANT water?

If you're stranded in the desert, and the sun is blazing hot, and you haven't had anything to drink for three days, do you NEED water, or do you WANT water?

What if you just got a brand new pool, and you want to go swimming? Need or want?

What if your car is really dirty?

What if you're a farmer, and there hasn't been rain in two weeks, and your crops are dying?

Acts 3:1-7

Psalm 41

1 John 3:1-7

Luke 24:36b-48

Keywords
Need
Want
Water

What if you were a fish?
Feel free to add your own to the list!
You see, there are times when we want something and other times when we need something. God knows what our wants and our needs are, and God will give us what we need.

Fourth Sunday of Easter

Acts 4:5-12

Psalm 23

1 John 3:16-24

John 10:11-18

Message

What we look like on the outside is not as important as who we are on the inside.

Commentary

All of the readings today remind us that looks are deceiving. What may appear to be the truth may in fact be false and vice versa. In the Acts passage Peter and John appeared before the religious leaders of the day to justify their miracles. They repeated a common phrase said about Jesus: "The stone that was rejected by you, the builders; it has become the cornerstone" (Acts 4:11). Jesus did not look like the Messiah to the leaders. They rejected him, yet he became the cornerstone of faith in God. In the Gospel, Jesus spoke of a good shepherd and a hired hand. The shepherd was sincere in his care for the sheep. The hired hand had no real interest in the flock and so ran when the going got tough. Only the good shepherd had the commitment to lay "down his life for the sheep" (John 10:11). Jesus is the good shepherd. Then in the first letter of John, we read that true love for our neighbor is seen in our inner being and not just in our words. We are to show love in our actions, and then we "know that we are from the truth" (1 John 3:19).

Story: SOCCER IT TO ME

In this story we play up the contrast between the beautiful and the plain. We use a soccer ball and a balloon. An old, dirty, scuffed-up, frayed soccer ball is best for the contrast against a beautiful and pretty balloon. Part of the trick is to

52

have a small pushpin or sewing pin concealed in your hand while you go through this story.

Kick around the soccer ball in the sanctuary for a few minutes. If you are not allowed to do this in your conservative church (or if you're just not gutsy), at least have the ball in hand to explain to the children what it is for. Let one of the kids give it a good wallop. If you're brave or have an understanding congregation, go down the aisle with the ball and let one or two of the kids kick it back and forth. Comment on how much fun the soccer ball can be, even if it is a little tattered and torn.

Blow up the beautiful big balloon and let the kids bop it around between them for a few tries. Even in stodgy cathedrals you should be able to get away with this. After the balloon has been around a bit and comes back to you, allow it to touch the pin and pop. When we do this, sometimes one of the more perceptive children will realize we popped the balloon with a pin. That's OK; when it happens, we usually incorporate their comments into the talk below.

We learn that most of the time in our lives the outward appearance of things is wrong. What we are really made up of is shown when things get difficult for us. The soccer ball did not look very pretty or fancy, but it took a lot more rough play from us. The balloon was nice, but was not made of much, so it took a very little touch to make it pop. How about us? Will we pop like the flimsy, yet beautiful balloon, or will we withstand the tests like the well-worn soccer ball? Many times it may seem like it's difficult to be a Christian, to talk to our friends about Christ, to do good deeds for people. If we are strong Christians, we might not look pretty, but we will be able to stand up for what we believe and do good things.

Keywords

Appearances
Balloons
Christian love
Endurance
Soccer ball
Strength

You will need:
Soccer ball
Balloon
Pin

Fifth Sunday of Easter

Message

As Christians we know the call to pass the message of Christ's gospel along. We are the ones who have to do this.

Commentary

Evangelism is one of the important functions of the children of God. We are the ones called upon to bring the story of Christ and God's love to the world.

Philip was called to witness to a stranger on the road. Through this encounter the Ethiopian believed in Christ. Although it is not included in the story, we can assume the man went back to his home in Ethiopia and told others of the Good News he had received from Philip. The psalmist sings of how all the earth shall come to know God, all nations and all generations. How are they to know about this wonderful news if the Christians do not spread the word? In the passage in First John so much is said about love that it starts to sound repetitive, but the crux of the message is that God's love is seen in the love that is shown by those who have God's love in them. The Gospel of John explains that God's love abides in us, and it is expected that God's love be multiplied through our acts of love in this world: "My Father is glorified by this, that you bear much fruit and become my disciples" (John 15:8).

We are the bearers of the Good News to a waiting world. How do we get that news across?

Story: ALL THE NEWS YOU WANT TO HEAR

We make this story fun by collecting a bunch of the far-fetched tabloid newspapers from the local supermarket. The more outlandish the story, the better. Try to find stories that do not insult any particular person or social group. Every week at least one tabloid has an alien sighting. It might even be a bonus if you find a tabloid that announces the Messiah has been found in some obscure village in Antarctica. Have fun with this part. Also collect a couple of the mainstream newspapers from your area and have a Bible handy.

When the children have gathered, ask them where they get news or information about things. Some will say they learn things at school. Very few children read the newspapers, although some may catch some news on television or on the radio. Even if the children do not read the newspapers, they will likely know what one is, since they are so prevalent in our culture. If there is some significant current event, ask the children how they found out about it. Work at it until one of the children suggests the newspaper. If no one does, steer the conversation in that direction.

Show the children some of the newspapers you have collected and brought to church today.

Some of these newspapers have very reliable sources, and you know you can trust what they say. Some of these newspapers have stories that leave you a bit suspicious of their truth. Regardless of their stories, every newspaper is written for the purpose of getting news out to the people.

Ask the children what method they think is best for getting the news about Jesus Christ out to the world. Explain that the best newspaper we have about Jesus Christ and God is the Bible. Show the children that the Bible you have is full of stories about God's love that must be shared.

How do we get the news out about God? It is up to us, the Christians, to tell people. We are God's newspapers, and we must live, work, and do good deeds in the world so that everyone who sees us will see the love of God.

You will need:
Tabloid
  newspapers
Bible

Sixth Sunday of Easter

Message

As Christians we know the call to pass the message of Christ's gospel along. We are the ones who have to do this.

Commentary

During a visit to a Gentile family, Peter explained the gospel of Jesus Christ. This visit taught Peter more than it taught the family of Cornelius, as he stated his new understanding that God would no longer show partiality for the Jews, but that the Good News is for all people. In the passage for today the Holy Spirit moved, and it was clear to the believers present that they could not expect the Spirit to act according to their understanding. As this Sunday often falls on Christian Family Sunday or Mothers' Day, the family image is very easy to incorporate into the children's story. The Holy Spirit fills our families in the same way it fills our churches and ourselves.

In the psalm of praise all the earth is encouraged to sing new songs to the Lord.

Acts
10:44-48

Psalm 98

1 John
5:1-6

John
15:9-17

The First John passage has wonderful imagery of the believers being children of God. If we love God, we love others who are also the children of God. All this talk about children and love is wonderfully appropriate for a Christian Family Sunday. It is the Spirit of God that fills us and makes us capable of the love of God's children.

The Gospel of John continues to bear out this theme of God's love abiding in us. Our whole being — spirit, mind, and body — are fulfilled in this.

Story: OVERFLOWING WITH LOVE

As mentioned in the commentary section, if this Sunday falls on Mothers' Day, it is a simple connection between the family in Acts and the "love and abide" terminology in First John and the Gospel of John. If this is the case, make the connection plain during the following story. If it is not Mothers' Day, then this story becomes a great story about the abundance of God's love.

Ask the children, "Who do you love?" Ask them to point out someone in the congregation whom they love. Have the children go to that person whom they love and bring that person forward to join you at the front of the church. Mention that it would be OK for each child to bring forward more than one person. When you have a crowd of people at the front of the church, point out that not only are these new people loved by these children but that you are also pretty certain the children are loved by the new people.

There are so many people in this crowd that it is almost impossible to fit everyone at the front of our church. Well, that abundance of people is a good example of God's abundance of love for us. Just like we are overflowing with people who love one another here, God is overflowing with love for us. In the Bible readings today we are reminded that God's love abides in us, but it also overflows from us to other people. Let us thank God for all this love we can share in our families and in our friendships, and let us thank God that it all starts with God's love abiding in us.

Message

Each one of us is special and unique. God chooses each one of us individually, not because of who our parents are, or what church we go to, or what we look like. God knows what's inside us.

Acts
1:15-17,
21-26

Psalm 11

1 John
5:9-13

John
17:6-19

Commentary

The prayer of Jesus in the Gospel of John leaves no doubt that the twelve apostles were not random choices. They were given to Jesus by God for their talents and abilities. Even Judas was chosen to be part of this brotherhood. We know they were not the only ones who followed Jesus. There were many others at the fringes, but these twelve were special. So too was Matthias chosen to fill Judas' place. By drawing lots, the disciples again looked for God's will in choosing who would take his place.

The practice of drawing lots for leadership positions is not uncommon in some churches today. It is founded on the belief that God chooses leaders in God's way and time. The psalmist reinforces that trusting in God is better than trying to take things into our own hands. Try and run, and the arrow of the wicked will find you. God chooses us if we let ourselves be chosen. And that's the trick, isn't it? You can't make someone love you. You can only make yourself available to be loved. We can't make God do anything. We can only make ourselves available to be chosen.

Story: YOU WILL CHOOSE ME

This is a great illusion that will leave the congregation mesmerized. The point will be reinforced especially well if you don't spill the beans on how you did it. Have five identical envelopes. We like to use envelopes made from recycled paper. We're not trying to be environmentally conscious, although that's a good thing, but the flecks on the paper make it easier for you to hide your "mark." That's right, you need to secretly mark one envelope so that you can distinguish it from the other four. Place a sheet of paper in the marked envelope that says in large letters: "You will choose me." On each of four other sheets of paper write one of the following words: "You"; "won't"; "choose";

Keywords
Call
Chosen
Disciple
Envelope

"us." *Place one sheet of paper into each of the other four envelopes. Close all the envelopes without sealing them. Now you are ready. Speak to the children along these lines:*

When we think about all the people God has called to work in the kingdom, it's amazing to think how God knows what each person can do, and what role he or she needs to play. You see, God knows what's in your heart. God searches your heart and calls you to be the kind of person that you ought to be. Some are called to be disciples, some are called to be teachers, some are called to be plumbers, and so on. Now I need five helpers for a little demonstration. I want each of you to take an envelope. Take any one you like and stand in a row here where everyone can see you. But don't open your envelopes! (*IMPORTANT: Make sure you know which child has the marked envelope.*)

The rest of the selection process involves a number of "forces," to use card trick language. You are going to force your next two helpers to leave the child with the marked card standing alone. Ask one of the other children (one not holding an envelope) to go behind the five and tap any two on the head. If she taps the one with the marked envelope, say, "She has chosen you two; the other three may sit down, but don't open your envelopes." If she taps the two who don't have the marked envelope, say, "She has chosen you two to sit down." Now you have either two or three children standing. Ask another child to go up and take the hand of any two children. If she holds the hand of the one with the marked envelope, send the third one away. Now she is holding two children's hands. Ask her to let go of one. If she lets go of the one with the marked envelope, tell her to take the person whose hand she is holding and go sit down. If she lets go of the other's hand, tell her to stand beside the person she has chosen. Ask the one remaining to open her envelope, read it to the congregation, and show it to them. Here's the kicker: Pretend to begin to collect the other envelopes, and then pause as if someone said something to you.

Pardon, you think it says that in everyone's envelope? I'm sorry, I got caught. I thought I could fool you, but you're a little sharper than I thought. Come on, you other four. Come up here and show everyone what it says in your envelope.

As they open their envelopes, arrange them so that the whole congregation can read the four words, "You won't choose us."

We do not know how God knows what's inside of us. All we know is that God knows what's inside of us. And God will choose each one of us because of who we are inside.

Pentecost and After

Day of Pentecost

Message

The Holy Spirit blows where it will, and we have to go where it takes us.

Commentary

The focus for Pentecost Sunday is, of course, the Holy Spirit. The readings for this day reflect this, and most of the Scripture passages are the same throughout the three years of the lectionary cycle.

It is the Holy Spirit that gave the disciples courage and inspiration to preach in the Acts passage. The psalmist gives credit to the Holy Spirit for the creation and renewal of the natural order. The prophet Ezekiel was often taken "by the Spirit of the LORD" to places of ecstatic vision; in the vision of the dry bones, it was not until the bodies were infused with the breath or spirit of God that they took on life. The Gospel passage has Jesus promising his followers that the Holy Spirit would come to them after he was gone.

The Holy Spirit is an integral part of our church and our individual lives. How do we see it moving in our world?

Story: BLOWING THROUGH THE CHURCH

As mentioned in the commentary section the readings for today are similar for all three years of the lectionary cycle. We wanted to use much the same illustration this year as in Year A, but with a fun twist. You'll need lots of balloons. As well as having a bunch of balloons for the children gathered at the front, we branched out with this one and placed balloons in the pews before the service started.

Ezekiel 37:1-4

Psalm 104:24-35b

John 15:26-27; 16:4b-15

Acts 2:1-21

Keywords
Balloons
Holy Spirit

Explain to the children that Pentecost Sunday is our celebration of the Holy Spirit coming to the disciples.

Once they had been inspired, they went out and told the world about Jesus Christ. This was surprising since they were not very good public speakers. People who heard them, though, were amazed to hear them in many different languages so that all the world could understand. If you had told any one of the disciples a year before that he would do this, he would have said you were crazy. But the Holy Spirit can give us inspiration to do amazing things.

Ask the children where they think the Holy Spirit might take them in their life. Try this. Have them blow up the balloons, one for each child. Ask the older children to please help the younger children. Do not have them tie the end of the balloon, but rather hold the end closed tightly in their fingers. Ask them to stand and hold their balloons high in the air and comment on how pretty this makes the church look — filled with all these balloons.

Now say that if they want to know what the Holy Spirit may do with their lives, they should let their balloon go. The resulting scene is as close as we can get to a fireworks display indoors. It is always gorgeous to see a church filled with multicolored balloons tthhpppting around the room as the air is released. They go all over in every direction. If the whole congregation is involved, this is accompanied by many oohs and aahs, much like a fireworks display.

The point to make is that as the breath (spirit) has filled these balloons and made them go in all sorts of unexpected directions, when we are filled with God's Spirit, we can expect to be taken in all sorts of unexpected directions as we let God's Spirit flow from us.

Message

There are a lot of us who make up the church. Everyone is different, and everyone is needed.

Isaiah 6:1-8

Psalm 29

Romans 8:12-17

John 3:1-17

Commentary

Romans 8:12-17 is good for a children's story with the way it calls Christians "children of God." We are God's children, but not by the way that most of us are children of our parents. God has adopted us as children. There may be some children in your group who have been adopted, and this image is rich as it tells that adopted children, although not born into the family, are just as loved and cared for as biological children. A caution here, though, is to be aware that many of our traditional nursery stories and tales have bad images of adopted relationships. Cinderella and Hansel and Gretel suffered a lot in their adopted relationship. The bottom line of these stories is, however, to tell us that those relationships were wrong. Things that are wrong are supposed to be set right, hence the other two stories.

The Isaiah passage is the dramatic calling of a prophet of the Lord. What it took from Isaiah was the recognition that he and his society were unclean, following by a fixing by a fiery coal. This story is in the form of a vision, a dream. Don't let children believe that Isaiah had an actual coal placed on his mouth.

In Jesus' talk with Nicodemus, Jesus makes it certain that we must change from one thing into another when we become Christian. Everyone born of the Spirit is like a new thing. Something old is new again, but as in the case of Christ himself, there is often some terrible trial to make that change.

Keywords
Change
Cookies
Goop
Heat
Trial

Story: COOKIE DOUGH CHRISTMAS

For this story have all the ingredients for your favorite chocolate chip cookies, a bowl to mix them in, and some homemade chocolate chip cookies. Make them yourself, even if you're a lousy cook. It will mean something to the congregation to have the minister go to some extra effort for this children's time, even if the result is not as good as Mrs. Fields.

Ask if any of the children have ever helped their parents make chocolate chip cookies. Some of them probably have. Ask if they would like to help you make some now because you have all the stuff needed for the cookies, and wouldn't it be nice if we could all enjoy some? Mix the ingredients together in front of them. Be expressive with breaking the eggs. Before you put the chocolate chips in, make sure the children all see the goopy, ugly mess. Ask them if they want the chips to go in this mess, or if they'd rather have them without the mess. Put them in anyway and show the kids what an ugly thing the cookie batter is.

(Some of the kids may want to taste the raw batter, but because of food poisoning related to raw eggs, we do not recommend it.) Ask them if they know what is missing that would make this goop into cookies. Most of them will know that it has to be baked. Describe baking as putting this stuff under very high heat for a long time. Then present them with some homemade cookies made from the same recipe and explain that this is what happens to the goop after it has been baked. It changes from this mess to this delicious treat.

God wants beautiful things in God's world. Our lives might be messy at times, or we might feel we are going through some really hard and tough times, but through this, God is creating good things — us.

Second Sunday After Pentecost

Message

Big or small, God uses us all. It's what's inside our hearts that counts.

Commentary

The story in First Samuel about the calling of Samuel makes for a great children's story. A child is the main character; and as in most of our children's movies today, the story makes the adults look rather foolish and out of touch. It is good for us adults to get the message every now and then that God calls anyone God wants, and sometimes it is the unexpected child or outcast or marginalized people whom God wants.

In the psalm we are reminded that God knows every intimate detail about us, so God is in a pretty good position to know what we can or cannot do. From the Gospel story of the grain plucking and hand healing, we get the message that God is expecting us to live by the spirit of the law and not the restrictive detail, most of which is human generated. God will do what God wants in order to heal and help, even if that means going against our rules.

Paul's letter to the Corinthians gives us a good image to take into the children's story. He talks about the treasure we hold in clay jars. The jars, our bodies, are fragile and short-lived, but inside these jars is kept a treasure, God's love.

1 Samuel
3:1-20

Psalm
139:1-6,
13-18

2 Corinthians
4:5-12

Mark
2:23–3:6

Story: TREASURES IN CLAY JARS

You will need:
Treasure
candy

Have at least one sample of a toy or candy that is known for having some special prize inside. Cracker Jack is one example, but my favorite is the Kinder Egg; it offers a great example of breaking open some weak item to reveal a treasure inside.

Explain to the children as you're breaking and opening the candy that the weak outer shell is easy to crush, easy to destroy, but what is important is the prize that waits for us inside.

Keywords
Candy
Clay jars
Fragile
Treasure

That is similar to our faith in Jesus. We may be weak and frail humans. We may not be the best at sports, like Michael Jordan or Tiger Woods is. We may get sick and even break a leg or an arm sometime in our lives. That's natural.

What is important to God is what is in our hearts — what we think and how we love and care. This is the treasure that God cares about in us, even if it is kept in a weak and breakable person. Always remember that to God it's what's inside you that matters, not how you look or what you can do.

1 Samuel
8:1-22

Psalm 138

2 Corinthians
4:13–5:1

Mark
3:20-35

Keywords

Christ
Following
Leaders
Toys

Message

We choose who will have dominion in our lives. We must choose well.

Commentary

This is one of those lectionary Sundays that is all chopped up with options for the worship leader. For the purposes of this story we are recommending the whole of 1 Samuel 8 be read, as it all deals with quality leadership. In this passage the people are demanding that God appoint a king over them so that they can be "like other nations." It seems like a reasonable request, given the descriptions of Samuel's heirs in verse 3. But Samuel realized the danger of their request. He served up a pretty accurate warning of what would happen to the nation under a king. Much of it holds true today. Samuel and God commiserated with each other about the request and in the end agreed that the time had come to choose a king to lead Israel. The choice of that king had to be made carefully and wisely. The following chapters offer a variable picture concerning this development.

The question of Jesus' leadership is challenged in the Gospel reading. Even his own family seemed to have doubts about his sanity, and many others were bringing accusations against him concerning his authority or sincerity in his miracles. These were serious concerns. People are unlikely to follow a rabbi with bad credentials. All of the arguments against him were dealt with, however, and history makes it clear to us that Jesus was the right one to follow.

Story: FOLLOW THE LEADER

Bring a toy that includes several units connected together to be towed along or that move along under battery power. The longer, the better. A toy train is a good example. I have seen a string of toy ducklings connected together, with a mother duck at the front. Demonstrate the toy, showing that all the parts of the toy follow the leader; because of this, no matter where the leader goes, they will all end up at the same place.

Usually this is a good thing. The train cars all want to get to the same train station. The baby ducklings would be in trouble if they ever ended up separated from their mother. But what would happen if the lead train went to the wrong stations for some reason? Then all the cars end up in the wrong place because they all had to follow the same leader.

It is important in our Christian lives that we know which leaders we are going to follow — which leaders are the right ones to follow. That can be a hard decision sometimes because lots of leaders look good at first and then we might find out they are bad leaders. One leader we know we can always trust, who will never lead us to the wrong place, is Jesus Christ. If you have to follow someone or something, always remember the things that Jesus taught us and the things he asked us to do as his followers. In the end his leadership will always be good for us.

Fourth Sunday After Pentecost

Message

The Lord makes it happen.

Commentary

It's a good thing that God sees us not as we see ourselves, or how many of us would stand up to our own scrutiny, or rather, the way we scrutinize others? When Jesse brought his sons before Samuel, Samuel was at first impressed by Eliab, but God said, "Do not look on his appearance or on the height of his stature, because I have rejected him; for the LORD does not see as mortals see; they look on the outward appearance, but the LORD looks on the heart" (1 Samuel 16:7). We know we breathe a sigh of relief that we're not judged by our looks. Although we have to admit, being judged by the content of our hearts gives us the willies as well. However, God sees inside

1 Samuel 15:34—16:13

Psalm 20

2 Corinthians 5:6-10, (11-13), 14-17

Mark 4:26-34

our hearts, our motives, our dreams, and our ideals. This is a sobering thought for a pastor. Nevertheless, we take heart in the fact that God does work with us in spite of our imperfections. Moreover, this is what we should focus on, that God is at work, not us. Although the farmer in the parable may scatter the grain or plant the mustard seed, it is God who does the actual work, not us. Our place is to have courage and walk by faith, not trusting in our own sight. Nor, as the psalmist puts it, should we boast of chariots or horses. It is through faith in God that we will rise and stand upright.

Keywords
Blindfold
Faith
Trust

Story: BLIND TRUST

Many times we talk of trusting God to guide us, but it's a hard thing to imagine, even for grownups. God wants us to trust the Holy Spirit and to follow in the footsteps of Jesus, but that takes a lot of trust. I'd like to play a little game here to show you what it means to be trusting and to be guided by someone. I have a blindfold here for each of you. I want you to put them on. Make sure you can't see anything. (*You might want to have a few helpers to put them on.*) Now we're going to take a walk. Everyone hold hands. I'm not going to take you anyplace dangerous or anyplace where you might get hurt. My eyes are wide open, and I'm watching out for you. I even have some helpers who will be walking near you to help you if you get into trouble.

Take the children on a walk around the sanctuary, or the church; you may even take them outside. Have fun with this. When you get back, have them take the blindfolds off.

Did it feel uncomfortable not knowing where you were going or what was coming next? Were you able to relax and trust the person who was leading you, or the person who was following? You know, the way you felt is very similar to how God's people have felt for thousands of years. It's learning to trust God, even though we don't know where we're being led, that's one of the hardest things in the world to do. But we can do it.

You will need:
Blindfolds

Message

Salvation is in God's hands, even if you do not recognize God's hands.

Commentary

The story of David and Goliath is a good way to teach the power of God. In this young boy's action, we are shown that human might and power does not make right. Instead, David with the power of God on his side was able to overcome Goliath. How often have we seen people in our own churches using their money, power, or position to have their way? How often have the clergy done the same thing? (You may now shift uncomfortably in your chair.) But, as is God's way, the most unlikely of characters is used to show that God's power overcomes the powers of this world.

Even the wind and the sea can be overcome by the power of God in the spoken words of Jesus. This is not magic; this is God showing the disciples that even those things that seem impossible to control are in God's hands. If you have ever encountered a storm on the open sea, you can attest to the terrifying effects of wind and wave. Both of us have logged many hours in canoes and have seen our share of wind and wave. In a boat loaded down with equipment or people, the effect of the elements is heightened, as the boat does not respond at all.

Trust in God, even in the face of the truly unstoppable forces of this world. You will see God's salvation find its way to you, often in the least likely of ways.

Story: ABRAM THE ROPE MAKER

As you tell this story, you will have three strings in your hands: one long, folded double, and two short. Keep shuffling them together and pulling them apart; it will appear that you have four pieces of string, and you will look like the thoughtful Abram in the story. Feel free to change the gender of the main character to suit yourself. Find the middle of the long string, and

1 Samuel 17:(1a, 4-11, 19-23), 32-49

Psalm 9:9-20

2 Corinthians 6:1-13

Mark 4:35-41

You will need:
Three pieces of household string: two about two feet long, one four feet long

twist it so that the strands separate. Take half of the strands and twist them; they will look like the end of the string. Do the same with the other half. When you let the string hang, with you holding onto these fake ends, it will appear like you have two strings in your hands. Now hold the other strings. "VOILA!" — it appears as if you have four strings of equal length. As you talk about Abram and shuffle the strings back and forth, you will create an effect where it appears that you indeed have four separate strings. When you discard the two short strings, you will be ready for this simple, but effective, illusion.

The story is told on the banks of the Jordan River of a simple rope maker named Abram. Abram would spend days sitting and making ropes as his father before him did, and his father before him. As Abram had a lot of time to himself as he worked diligently with his hands, he did a lot of thinking. People came to respect the wisdom of Abram. They knew if they had a problem, they could go to Abram.

One day news came to the village that a violent gang of travelers was coming towards the village, and they were going to destroy everything and kill everyone. The people came to Abram and pleaded for help. Surely he could think of a way to keep their village from being destroyed.

One person suggested they make themselves into an army and build weapons with which to fight. "No," said Abram softly. "Hands are for helping, not for hurting." Another suggested that Abram make a rope so strong they could tie up the evil gang and throw them off a cliff! "No," said Abram softly. "Hands are for helping, not for hurting." "Then what will we do?" the people cried. "Let me think about it until morning," said Abram, and he worked with his ropes through the night.

The next morning as the gang of ruffians approached the village, Abram left his shop and took with him a couple of pieces of rope. (*Put the two shorter pieces aside, holding the long piece so that it still appears to be two pieces.*)

The town followed Abram as he went to the edge of the village and waited for the intruders. When the intruders arrived, they were bigger, meaner, and nastier than even the rumors had said. Abram sat patiently and waited for the leader to speak.

"I challenge the strongest man in your village to a fight," the leader said. "If he defeats me, we will leave. But if he doesn't, we will tear apart your village and take what we want."

Abram waited as the many strong men in the village slowly shuffled to the back of the crowd, because they were afraid.

Keywords

David
Goliath
Salvation
String

Then he spoke. "I will challenge not only you, but also your strongest man to a feat of strength," said Abram. He continued, "I have more strength in my thumb and forefinger than either of you have in your entire bodies." At this, the whole gang laughed out loud. "Very well," said the leader. "Let us begin."

Select two small children to act the part of the ruffians. Give each one an end of the string, while you hold the other two "ends" between your thumb and forefinger. You will be able to wrap the rest of your hand around the string to conceal the effect. Tell the children to start pulling slowly; if they pull too quickly, the string may break. As you feel the string pull taut, you can remove your hand to the amazement of all.

And when Abram removed his hand, he said very softly, "Hands are for helping, not for hurting." The ruffians were so amazed at the power of Abram that they left quickly, muttering among themselves long into the night about the strange thing they had seen.

Sixth Sunday After Pentecost

Message

God hears our cries and looks after our needs. In addition, we ought to hear the cries of others and look after their needs.

Commentary

In Psalm 130 we hear the pitiful cry of one waiting for God's salvation, a cry wrapped in hope and trust that God will rescue. As we read the interesting stories of healing in the Gospel of Mark, we find that while both are healings by faith, when placed side by side there is a marvellous difference. Both Jarius and the woman who was suffering from a twelve-year hemorrhage sought out Jesus. Jarius sought him out and pleaded face to face, "Come and lay your hands on (my daughter)" (Mark 5:23). He sought an act from Jesus that would bring healing to his daughter. The woman, on the other hand, sneaked up on Jesus, believing, "If I but touch his clothes, I will be made well" (verse 28). Jesus

2 Samuel
1:1, 17-27

Psalm 130

2 Corinthians
8:7-15

Mark 5:21-43

healed both, and there is the beauty of these two stories. Whether you come to Jesus and plead face to face, or sneak up behind him and reach out in faith, Jesus will respond to your act of faith.

Paul in Second Corinthians exhorts the reader to respond to the needs of others because they have faith. Faith requires action. Paul complimented the Corinthians on their faith, their knowledge, and their love. Then Paul pushed them to excel in their acts of charity. Therefore, faith in Jesus allows us to reach out to Jesus however we choose, and faith in Jesus should also cause us to reach out our hand to those around us who need our help.

Keywords

Hands
Helping
Faith

Story: TWO GOOD HANDS

Take a look at your hand for a moment. It is one of God's most wonderful creations. Did you know that there are twenty-seven bones in your hand? You have eight carpal bones; these are the little ones at your wrist. Next are five metacarpal bones; these are the long skinny ones you can feel in the back of your hand. Then there are phalanges; these are all the little bones that make up your fingers and thumb. That's twenty-seven bones all together, and look at all the wonderful things your hand can do. You can touch your thumb to any finger, you can wiggle it, you can wave it, and you can pick things up. You can hold a pen and write your name. You can juggle, you can throw a ball, you can catch a ball. You can scratch an itch or rub your eyes. (You shouldn't pick your nose, but your hand can do it, if it needs to be done.) You can reach your hands high into the air and wave at your parents. You can pat your friend on the back or hold hands, if you want to.

Isn't it wonderful that you have two hands? It's not like one is a spare, in case the other wears out. You use both your hands all the time. Some people use one hand more than the other. Some people are right-handed. Who here is right-handed? Who is left-handed? Some people are ambidextrous — that means they can do things with either hand.

Do you know what I like to think my two hands are for? I like to think one hand is the one I reach up to God with when I need help. Have you ever reached up to your parents for them to pick you up, or to help you? Well, that's what you do when you need help from God. You lift one hand up to God, and God, like a loving parent, will reach down and take your hand. The other hand, well, that's for reaching out to someone else who needs help. If you ever see someone who is hurt or sad, then you take your other hand and reach out to him or her. One hand is for reaching for God. The other is for reaching out for the people who need help. You have two good hands: God wants you to use both of them.

Seventh Sunday After Pentecost

Message

God's power is manifested in the weak and the unlikely.

2 Samuel
5:1-5, 9-10

Psalm 48

2 Corinthians
12:2-10

Mark 6:1-13

Commentary

The passage in Second Samuel tells of David being anointed king over Israel. David, the once small shepherd boy, had been made king. The people recognized that it was not David's doing that he was able to lead them, but rather God's presence in David's life. This is God's way, using the weak and the unlikely to demonstrate the power of the Spirit. Were God to use the strong and the mighty, where would be the place for God to be exalted?

Turning to the Gospel of Mark we are left wondering why Jesus could do no mighty work in his hometown. Is it that he was powerless? Not by any means. It is rather because they did not believe in him and so did not seek out his help. They saw in him the carpenter they had known. Their eyes were closed to the changes he had been through, and they were not able to accept Jesus in his new role. Perhaps this is a good thing; had the people who had known him all rallied around him, the groundswell of support would have turned him into a local hero in a way that would have drawn the focus away from the gospel he was preaching.

Paul acknowledges in Second Corinthians that God needs to hamstring us a little in order to keep us humble and focused on giving credit for what we do to God. This is at the heart of the difference between those that would build God's Kingdom and those who would build their own empires. By using the unlikely and the weak, God's power is made evident to the world.

Story: TELEMACHUS

Keywords

Gladiator

Telemachus

Weak

About 1600 years ago, there was a man named Telemachus. He was a monk and lived in a monastery. One day he felt something telling him to go to Rome. He knew it was God, and although he didn't know why God would send him to Rome, he obeyed. Packing a few things and taking a little food, he set out on foot to Rome.

When he arrived in Rome, Telemachus was impressed. It was the biggest city he had ever seen. There was so much commotion, so many things to see. Telemachus still did not know why God wanted him to come to this place, but he figured God would let him know. He followed the crowds and wandered through the city. The people seemed to be streaming to a big huge stadium. He tried to stop a few passersby and ask them what was going on, but everyone was in a hurry. They wanted to get the best seats possible.

Finally Telemachus got a nice young man to tell him what the big event was. "Don't you know?" the young man asked. "Today the gladiators are fighting. There will be fights, wild animals, blood, and everything. Come on. You'd better hurry, or you won't be able to see anything."

Telemachus had never seen a gladiator, so he followed the young man and the crowd into the stadium. Telemachus marveled at the size of the stadium and the party atmosphere. There were thousands of people laughing, chatting, and having a marvelous time. Telemachus thought about the feeling that he had at the monastery. Why did God want him here? Maybe he was supposed to go somewhere else in Rome.

He was about to leave when the first two gladiators came into the stadium. They raised their swords and shields, and the crowd went wild. Telemachus watched in horror as he realized what was going to happen. These two men were going to fight to the death for the amusement of these people. He looked beside him at the young man who was cheering and yelling, waiting to see one of them be killed by the other.

Telemachus thought, "These men should not be killing each other. This is not entertainment. This bloodlust is wrong!" Without a thought for his own safety, Telemachus leapt to his feet and ran down the steps of the stadium. He struggled over the wall and dropped onto the dirt floor of the stadium. The gladiators were circling each other, waiting to see who would find a weakness and strike first.

Telemachus ran toward them. When the crowd saw him, some thought he was crazy. Others started laughing at the site of the little monk running towards the two hulking fighters. Telemachus stood in between them and raised his hands towards them. "In the name of Christ, stop!" he cried.

With a laugh one of the gladiators took his sword and swatted Telemachus in the stomach, sending him tumbling backwards into the dust. The roar of the laughing crowd filled his ears. Telemachus staggered to his feet, brushed himself off, stepped back between the two gladiators, and said again, "In the name of Christ, please stop!"

The laughter of the crowd turned to chanting as someone started yelling, "Run him through, run him through!" Louder and louder they yelled, until one gladiator took his sword and stabbed Telemachus in the stomach. Telemachus fell to the ground. As his life slipped away, he said one last time, "In the name of Christ, stop!" Then he breathed his last and died.

The chants evaporated as the crowd watched in silence. It seems that watching someone be killed was suddenly not very entertaining. The gladiators dropped their swords and stepped backwards. Slowly the hushed crowd filed out of the stadium.

And so it was that this was the last gladiatorial contest in the Roman Empire. A little monk hearing the call of God was able to bring to an end this brutal, horrible practice.

Eighth Sunday After Pentecost

Message

Things are sweeter with God in the mix.

Commentary

The story of King David bringing the Ark of the Covenant to Jerusalem has interesting elements to it. For the purposes of the children's time, the altercation with Michal may not be necessary. What we take from this story, though, for today's message is that wherever the ark resided, the household was

2 Samuel 6:1-5, 12b-19

Psalm 24

Ephesians 1:3-14

Mark 6:14-29

73

Keywords

Christ

Powdered
   drink mix

Sweet

blessed. There is no physical ark in our churches today, but the Ark of the Covenant can be taken to mean the presence of God. According to Exodus 25 God spoke to Moses from this ark during Israel's wandering years. With the presence of God in our midst, we know things will go better for us.

The psalm repeats that the righteous will receive blessings from the Lord. The blessing theme is chanted many times in the first verse of the Ephesians reading. The blessing talked about here is founded upon Christ and upon God's plan for the world's redemption through Christ.

We confess we don't really know what to do with the Gospel reading, as far as the children are concerned. It's unlikely that the beheading of John the Baptist can be used in this Sunday's story. For the adult sermon a connection may be made to the fact that Jesus had become so popular that even before the crucifixion and resurrection, people were already thinking of him as a great leader from their past returned from the dead.

Story: HOW SWEET IT IS

You will need:
Unsweetened
   drink mix
Sugar
Clear pitcher
Small cups

For this talk have a pitcher of water, a packet of powdered drink mix, and a cup of sugar handy. Do not use the pre-sweetened variety of drink mix. We always try to use a clear pitcher to add to the visual effect and color of the service. If it's possible in your situation to serve some of the drink to the children, have some small cups nearby.

When the children have gathered, ask if any of them have been feeling a bit thirsty today or if anyone thinks a nice cool cup of something to drink would brighten up church this morning. Well, you have something special for everyone. Bring out the powdered drink mix and mix it up in the pitcher, but omit the sugar.

Ask if anyone is ready to try a cup. Someone may remind you that it needs sugar. If you are not stopped, we leave it up to you as to whether or not you serve this stuff. If someone stops you, or if someone tastes the drink and winces, then admit that you made a mistake. Of course, you forgot to add the sugar.

You know, with the drink we can get the flavor and the color, and that's nice. But it needs sugar to make it sweet and enjoyable, doesn't it? We need Jesus Christ to make our lives sweet and enjoyable. Never forget to thank God for the way sugar makes our favorite drinks tasty. And never forget to be thankful that Jesus Christ came, and through his forgiveness our lives have been made enjoyable.

Message

People should be able to easily recognize us as God's children.

Commentary

While God had reasons for not allowing David to build a temple for the Ark of the Covenant, there is no doubt of God's continuing blessing upon David, as described throughout the second half of the Second Samuel passage. David believed God needed a house to live in, but God saw it differently. God wants to dwell in the home of the hearts and souls of God's people.

We are reminded in the Ephesians passage of the fact that we are all included in God's household because of Christ. It is not restricted to David's kingdom in time or nationality, nor is it dependent upon a temple or a specific location. While David wanted to build a stone temple for God's presence, we "are built together spiritually into a dwelling place for God" (Ephesians 2:22).

Jesus was a traveling rabbi. He had no specific house or home that he would return to each night after a hard day's work. We should see Christ's presence in our lives as an opportunity for us to make our hearts a home for Christ.

Story: IT'S NOT A HOUSE — IT'S A HOME

Bring along some pet homes or cages. This story is based upon birdhouses, but you can adjust this to make it work with hamster cages, aquariums, or bird cages — any small house that is a home to some pet or animal that is available to you.

Show the children what you have brought.

This is a birdhouse.

Maybe some of the children have some birdhouses in their yard, or perhaps they have seen these types of houses in other yards. This is an opportunity to talk with them about these little homes.

We make these boxes and put them up in the hopes that a pretty bird may come along and find that it is a nice place to

2 Samuel
7:1-14a

Psalm
89:20-37

Ephesians
2:11-22

Mark
6:30-34,
53-56

live. In this way we do something nice for the birds by giving them a nice place to live and raise their family of little birds. And they do nice things for us by showing off their pretty colors and singing their pretty songs in our neighborhoods.

It's nice to build these boxes and call them houses, but you know they are only special when the birds come to make them their homes. That makes a big difference. They go from being just boxes called houses to special places called homes.

It's like that for the places we live in too. We live in big huge boxes called houses. Until your family moved there, it was just an empty box called a house, an apartment, or a cottage. When you moved into the house and started living there and eating meals there and sleeping there and watching TV there and doing homework there and making noise and having fun there, that's when it became a home. It's no longer just a house on a street or an apartment in a building. It is your home.

Just like our homes and the birds' homes, our church is a home too. This big building is sometimes called God's house. But when God's people move into it and start living here and singing songs here and making noise here, then this becomes God's home. It's not just a big box, but a special place where people come to be at home with God. But this church is not where God stays all the time to be at home. You can make your homes God's home as well. If the place where you live is a place where people love one another, do good things for one another, and talk with God through prayer, then your houses and homes become homes for God. And that happens even at your school and at the places where you play and work. Whenever you are doing good things for others, you are making a place God's home.

Whenever you see these birdhouses, remember to think of them as a home when the birds move in. Whenever you go into your house, remember it is a home because you and your family live there. Whenever you come into this big place, remember it is a home for God's people. Always try to make other places like your home, your school, or your neighborhood a home for God too.

You will need:
Birdhouses

Message

Regardless of what we've seen God do for us, we are flawed creatures, and we forget God's place in our lives.

Commentary

Stunned. What more can one say after reading the account of David and Bathsheba? This was the great King David, who as a boy slew Goliath because God was on his side. This was the anointed one. How many times had David seen with his own eyes the power, might, and presence of God? David of all people ought to know what God had done for and with him! And yet a pretty girl made him forget all that. Whoosh, right out the window. When he could not cover up his transgression, he saw to it that her husband was killed. There you have it. The great King David involved in adultery and murder. (How's that for biblical family values?)

Jesus' disciples were a similar lot. No matter what they saw Jesus do, no matter what they heard Jesus teach, they seemed to forget who Jesus was showing himself to be. After Jesus fed a crowd of thousands with only five barley loaves and two fishes, and the leftover fragments filled twelve bushels, or when they saw Jesus approaching them on the water, they were afraid. All of Jesus' miracles seemed to be for naught when they were confronted with an unfamiliar situation. They forgot all the things that Jesus had said and done in their presence. David and the disciples forgot God's actions in their lives when confronted with their dilemmas.

Nevertheless, God continues to work with us flawed beings. As Paul writes, it is by the power of God that we are able to do far more than we could even conceive of. If only we could remember as each new situation arises what God has done for us and with us in the past.

Story: TELLING A STORY

On a flip chart write the following words: Telescope, Elephant, Tree, Jump, Slide, Tent, Ambulance, Chocolate, Pennsylvania, Camping. With the flip chart nearby speak to the children along these lines:

2 Samuel
11:1-15

Psalm 14

Ephesians
3:14-21

John 6:1-21

Keywords

Mnemonic
Remember
Story

One of the reasons we have a special time here at the front of the church is so we can tell stories. Sometimes I use a story to help you understand the Bible. Sometimes I use it to help the grownups understand what I'll be talking about later. But stories help us understand and remember things. Sometimes people can't remember a single thing I said all morning, but they remember a story I told. There are people who will never remember a single sermon, but they'll remember the stories that are told in them. That's why the Bible is such a wonderful teaching tool. It is full of stories that help us remember what God has done again and again and again. Then when we're confronted by something we haven't seen before, maybe we'll remember the stories of how God cares for us, and we will have faith and trust in God's will.

I want to show you ten words, and I want you to remember them all. (*Turn over the flip chart. Give the children a moment to read them, then cover them again.*) Okay, now tell me all the words in order. It's hard, isn't it? Some people have better memories than others; some people even can picture the list in their mind. But I'll show you an easy way to remember all those ten words without even seeing them again.

You will need:
Flip chart

Repeat after me. (*Do one line at a time. You may need to repeat it two or three times.*)

I was looking through my TELESCOPE.
I saw an ELEPHANT
Sitting in a TREE.
He was afraid to JUMP,
So he built a SLIDE.
He slid down into a TENT.
Inside the tent was an AMBULANCE.
It was made of CHOCOLATE.
The chocolate came from PENNSYLVANIA.
That's where I like to go CAMPING.

Now that these words are in a story, you can tell this story all the way home and whenever you're bored. That way you will never forget these words. That's why we keep telling stories about God — so we never forget.

Message

God wants us to be people of action, not passive recipients.

Commentary

The passage in Second Samuel is a favorite for those who like to dethrone the mighty, and well it should be. David committed not one but two reprehensible deeds. Nathan took a risk in calling him to task. Granted, his use of a parable was a wonderful teaching aid and helped David see himself as the perpetrator of this atrocity. (Kind of like using the children's story to get a difficult point across to your congregation. But we digress.) The point is, Nathan saw the need to act and committed himself.

In John the people were driven to pursue Jesus to get answers. They did not sit and wait for the gospel to be doled out to them, like a number of people in our pews these days. They chased Jesus down. They got boats and went after him. They questioned, they challenged, they wanted to know. These were people for whom seeking the bread of life was an active, not a passive, pursuit.

When Paul writes to the Ephesians about living a life "worthy of the calling," he is talking about an active, alive faith. Paul did not want the Ephesians to sit idly by. Everyone is given gifts, and we are to use those gifts with a purpose. We are told that it will take work and it will take resolve. Resolve like Nathan's, resolve like the people who doggedly pursued Jesus. Do we have the resolve to act, to take the risk, to commit ourselves to this pursuit?

Story: PEOPLE OF ACTION

We're going to play a game this morning. I've brought some pictures of people here, and I want you to look at them carefully. I know all of these people look different, but these people also have something in common; there is something that they all share.

Show the children the pictures. Some suggestions would be a firefighter, a police officer, someone from the Special Olympics, a lifeguard, a farmer, and so forth — anyone whose occupation or activity involves action and risk in a healthy, helping manner.

2 Samuel
11:26–12:13a

Psalm
51:1-12

Ephesians
4:1-16

John
6:24-35

Keywords

Action

Occupations

Risk

Have the children try to guess the connection. Try to have different ethnicities and both genders represented in the pictures.

What do all these people have in common? These are all people of action, people who take risks to accomplish great things. More than strength or endurance, they have heart. They believe in what they are doing, and they take action every day to accomplish what they must.

Now hold up the other pictures, the less identifiable people of action — a mother and child, a teacher, a plumber, a secretary, and so forth.

These are people of action too. Even though their jobs do not involve fires, exploding buildings, or high-speed chases, every day they put their beliefs into action in places where they work and play. God wants you to be people of action. You might be a firefighter, but you don't have to be. If you see someone hurting someone else, you can be a person of action and try to stop him or her. If you see someone hurt, you can be a person of action and help him or her. If you see some garbage on the ground, you can be a person of action, pick it up, and throw it away. Like the people in our story, you don't have to just sit in Sunday school and wait for the teacher to teach you. You can chase after the stories in your Bible, find out what's in there. You'll find out that God has wonderful things in store for you, if you jump in with both feet and your whole heart! Be a person of action!

12th Sunday After Pentecost

Message

We know we hurt one another and God. We need to reconcile with one another while we have the chance.

Commentary

No matter how old your child is, whether two years old or sixty-two years old, she is still your daughter. No matter how wicked and rebellious, he is still your son. The worst thing that can happen to parents is to have their children predecease them. We have learned as fathers and sons that our children do not feel about us the way we feel about them; they feel about us the way we feel about our parents. Likewise, our parents feel about us the way we feel about our children. This was an eye-opening revelation. David suffered the absolute anguish of losing his son. Although Absalom would have killed David if he had the chance, David ordered his servants to deal gently with him. David would have opened his arms to his rebellious son, but he never got the chance at reconciliation. He was left with a gaping emptiness in his heart and would have given his own life for his son's.

In the Gospel of John Jesus reveals that God has sent him as a sacrifice, his life in exchange for ours — so great is the love of a father or mother for his or her children. God is dealing with the same sort of rebellious children as David would, children that would kill the father, or his son, given the chance. Yet God longs for reconciliation, reconciliation before it is too late.

In the letter to Ephesians we are exhorted to walk in love with one another, to act in a way that does not distance us from one another. We are given specific examples of how to behave so that we do not begin to destroy the relationships we have with one another or with God. All too often it takes but a moment to cause incredible pain for someone we love, and then it takes a lifetime to heal from it. While the psalmist assures us that God does forgive us, what pain we endure waiting to forgive one another.

2 Samuel 18:5-9, 15, 31-33

Psalm 130

Ephesians 4:25–5:2

John 6:35, 41-51

Keywords

Apology
Feathers
Forgiveness

Story: FEATHERS IN THE WIND

In the Bible today we read about David's son Absalom dying. David's son behaved very badly, and we don't know if he would have ever made up with his father. But that didn't matter to David. When you love someone, it hurts very much when that person does things he or she shouldn't. When you behave badly, your parents hurt inside, and it's a very real hurt. Just like you hurt when someone you love does something to hurt you. Have you ever felt that pain inside your heart or your stomach when someone has hurt your feelings? Sometimes we feel bad about what we've done, and we say we're sorry. But just because we say we're sorry, that doesn't mean that the pain we caused isn't still there.

You will need:
Bag of feathers (or substitute confetti or rice)

Fan

Forgiveness from the custodian

Sometimes, like in the case of David and his son Absalom, we run out of time to say we're sorry, because someone dies or moves away. The things we say and do are like this bag of feathers. The wind from this fan is the passing of time. Every time we open our mouths, or do something to someone, we're opening a bag of feathers into the wind. Once they're scattered, we can never ever get them all back. We can try, but some will always be lost in the wind. That's why we should think before we speak and act. We should ask ourselves: Is what we're about to say or do loving or hurtful?

13th Sunday After Pentecost

1 Kings
2:10-12;
3:3-14

Psalm 111

Ephesians
5:15-20

John
6:51-58

Message

The fear of the Lord is the beginning of wisdom.

Commentary

"The fear of the LORD is the beginning of wisdom," says the psalmist in verse 10. That is a recurring theme throughout this Sunday's lectionary readings. Solomon was rewarded by God for seeking wisdom over riches and power. In granting wisdom God multiplied Solomon's greatness.

Ephesians reflects this truth by calling its readers to be careful in their lifestyles and to live wisely. It then goes into a series of "do's and don'ts" about what a wise life would include. We can't argue with the behaviors listed there.

One would expect to find wise teaching in the synagogue. When Jesus spoke there, he was challenged by the congregation, because his words seemed foolish to them. He talked about giving his flesh as the living bread that would bring eternal life. Although the theme of wisdom is not explicit in this passage, it is common in Jesus' teaching that human wisdom and God's wisdom are not always the same.

There is not much that needs to be said about the value of wisdom. We all know it, and we see it reflected in our Bible stories. We use this children's story to introduce the young people to the theme of wisdom in the Bible.

Story: WHO-WHO-WHOOO

A common image for wisdom in our culture is the owl. For this talk have a toy owl or a picture of an owl to help the children visualize the theme. Speak to them along these lines:

I was wondering who you people thought might be the smartest person in this church. Do you think the smartest person might be the choir director? Or perhaps the smartest person is your mum or dad. Does anyone here think you're the smartest person here? Who would say that I'm the smartest person here? After all, I do most of the talking, don't I?

Do you know of any very smart people in stories or in movies? Name some of the smartest people you know in stories or movies. Why do we say they are smart or wise? Many of the stories we read in school and at bedtime have an owl in them. They always say the owl is the wisest of all the creatures. Perhaps this is because an owl spends so much time just sitting calmly in a tree, and it looks like it is spending the whole day thinking and being wise. Or perhaps it is because when the owl speaks, it seems to be asking a question. The owl calls out, "Who, who, whooo," and it sounds like the owl wants to know more about who is nearby. We all know that a person becomes smart and wise by asking a lot of questions in order to learn a lot of things.

Do you know who God says is the wisest of all the creatures? In the Bible readings for today we are told that true wisdom comes from doing good things with God. True wisdom comes to us when we pray to God for wise decisions. True wisdom comes to us when we act properly with our friends and with ourselves. True wisdom comes to us when we remember that God is the source of our wisdom, and we praise God for the good things in our life.

When someone asks you who is the smartest person around or who is the smartest creature in the world, you can tell that person you know that true wisdom comes from our belief in God and from doing the things God wants us to do.

You will need:
An owl (model, toy, or picture)

Keywords
Owl
Wisdom

1 Kings
8:(1, 6,
10-11),
22-30,
41-43

Psalm 84

Ephesians
6:10-20

John
6:56-69

Keywords

Armor

Metaphor

Message

Put on the armor of God.

Commentary

Solomon made a long prayer at the dedication of the Temple. In the prayer he acknowledged that God would not necessarily dwell in that human construction, but that the Temple would come to be known as the place for God's name. People of all nations, not just the Jews, could come to this building and know about God, even if they would not see God's being. Prayer is essential in order to gain an understanding of God. This human creation, the Temple, would simply be a place where prayer could be focused, but not worshiped in and of itself. Over time, though, it seems the Temple did take on an element of its own deity.

The psalmist seems to declare the courts of the Lord as the best places to be. The worship of the Lord is the best occupation: "Happy are those who live in your house, ever singing your praise" (Psalm 84:4). Although we may look at these images in a metaphorical sense, it seems the writer had the physical building in mind.

Ephesians includes the description of the armor of God. This is a good illustration for the children's story, if we are careful. We believe the author was using the military image as a metaphor. There is no question in our minds that these instruments of war and violence were to be taken for war and violence. As is pointed out at the beginning of the passage, "our struggle is not against enemies of blood and flesh, but . . . against the spiritual forces of evil" (Ephesians 6:12). In this way the writer takes common articles of the time and uses them to evangelize. This is not much different than what we're trying to do with these books.

Consider the words of Jesus in the John passage. They are confusing. He uses phrases that border on cannibalism, but that was not his intent. It was his metaphor. His difficult imagery caused many disciples to turn away, but Peter confessed that these are still "the words of eternal life" (John 6:68).

Story: GOOD ARMOR

This story will take some preparation and collection of parts. We suggest you simply refer to the Ephesians passage and describe the armor as it is described there. There have been enough movies and television shows lately that dwell on medieval themes, so most of the imagery will be familiar. Collect each item listed in the Ephesians passage. You may be able find toy helmets (even a fire fighter's hat may work), plastic swords, and you can use your own leather belt as an illustration. Any items that are missing from your collection, such as a breastplate or a shield, can be made easily out of cardboard. Or perhaps these items can be borrowed from the high school drama department or the local community theatre troupe. Label each piece with the terms used in Ephesians (truth, righteousness, peace, and so forth).

As you present each item, be specific in asking the children what they might do to put on this armor. Ask, "In what ways can we be truthful?" as you put on the belt. Ask, "How will we use our shoes to bring peace?" You get the idea. This whole presentation may take a while, but there is nothing wrong with going overtime on the children's time with a well-prepared story. Do this right, and you cut the sermon time in half.

You will need:
Imitation armor

15th Sunday After Pentecost

Message

There are many things that block our hearing of God's Word. We must listen carefully through the rabble so that we will know how God wants us to live.

Commentary

Many times in Deuteronomy the writer prefaces the words with the exhortation to hear or to take special note of what follows. This passage is one example, but a more popular example is the Shema (Deuteronomy 6:4), which starts with the familiar "Hear, O Israel." In today's passage the writer is

Deuteronomy 4:1-2, 6-9

Psalm 45:1-2, 6-9

James 1:17-27

Mark 7:1-8, 14-15, 21-23

intent on getting the message across to the readers, because he knows how easy it is for distractions to take away from living out the message. As in the Shema these are things we must remember, because they must be made "known to your children and your children's children" (Deuteronomy 4:9).

In James' letter we are reminded to be "quick to listen, slow to speak, slow to anger" (James 1:19), but then are also told that hearing God's Word is only part of the plan. We must also take action on God's Word in our lives: "But be doers of the word, and not merely hearers who deceive themselves" (James 1:22). One who only listens to the word and takes no action on it can barely say he or she has heard the word at all.

You will need:
Earplugs

The Mark passage is chopped up, but throughout the sections the idea of listening up comes out. In verses 1-8 Jesus chastised the Pharisees for honoring God with their lips only. They had not listened to hear God's message of love for them. Jesus also used the same exhortation that we see in Deuteronomy, when in verse 14 he began his speech with the words, "Listen to me."

We must listen carefully to hear God's Word. Still, there are many things that keep the message from getting through to us.

Story: I CAN'T HEAR YOU

Show the children a pair of earplugs as you insert them in your ear. A more visual alternative would be the large ear covers, but these are harder to get. Explain to them that while you are wearing these plugs, you can't hear them talking or singing. If you're brave enough, give them the opportunity to scream out in church. You can smile blissfully while the rest of the congregation winces.

There are many things in our lives that can block out the words of the gospel so that the words cannot be heard. We should be careful that we do not do things that block out God's Word. Things like bragging, fighting, and arguing are loud things that prevent us from hearing. Things like anger and hatred can be quiet things that we keep inside but that still prevent us from hearing.

Always try to hear the good things that your teachers and your parents tell you about God and Jesus and our Christian life. Always be ready to remove anything from your lives that blocks out God's love. And then don't just listen to what God tells us, but be ready to do something about it too.

Message

The way God sees things, we are all the same.

Commentary

We usually dislike chopping up Scripture to fit a lectionary theme, but we have to admit that because of the nature of Proverbs, this is the best way. Today's snippets talk about equality between the rich and the poor. Proverbs 22:2 almost reads like a one-liner joke: "The rich and the poor have this in common: the LORD is the maker of them all." In verse 23 we are reminded that God cares for God's people, with no mention of their financial state.

In James' letter we are warned not to show partiality to people, based on their worldly goods. This passage repeats Jesus' words, "You shall love your neighbor as yourself" (James 2:8), then immediately adds, "But if you show partiality, you commit sin and are convicted by the law as transgressors" (verse 9).

Jesus did not show favor to financial groups or religious groups, it would seem. He did not even show much partiality when it came to known sinners. Jesus seems to be the most accepting rabbi around. In this story in Mark he extended his saving power to the Syrophoenician woman's family and then to a deaf mute from outside the Jewish faith. In the case of the Syrophoenician woman, there is dialogue concerning her worthiness, but we think this was included for the benefit of the disciples and perhaps for some comic sense. The woman turned out to be as capable as Jesus in turning a clever word to her advantage.

Story: NO DIFFERENCE

You might want to use the poem, "No Difference" by Shel Silverstein, or the Bette Midler song, "From a Distance," as a way to get across the message of acceptance and loving your neighbor.

Proverbs 22:1-2, 8-9, 22-23

Psalm 125

James 2:1-10, (11-13), 14-17

Mark 7:24-37

Keywords
Acceptance
Differences
Poem

Talk to the kids about the many ways we are alike and the many ways we are different, emphasizing that we are all brothers and sisters in Christ and therefore all children of God. It may be tempting to compare some children who are quite different from each other, but we don't recommend this because of the chance of hurt feelings. Talk about what it means to be created in the image of God. Then remind the children that God made people special and that Jesus saw everyone as a special child of God.

Each person in our church is special. Being special is a great responsibility. Being a special child of God — like Jesus — makes us responsible for loving as God loves and caring for God's world.

17ᵗʰ Sunday After Pentecost

Proverbs
1:20-33

Psalm 19

James
3:1-12

Mark
8:27-38

Message

Words are powerful tools. They must be used wisely.

Commentary

The Proverbs passage is all about wisdom, and here wisdom is brought to life as a woman crying in the streets. Wisdom is given words to appeal to any who will listen. Those who listen to wisdom "will be secure and will live at ease, without dread of disaster" (Proverbs 1:33). Psalm 19 gives similar instruction, except here "there is no speech, nor are there words . . . yet their voice goes out through all the earth, and their words to the end of the world" (Psalm 19:3, 4). The message in this wordless decree is that by following God's law, the simple become wise, and God's wisdom is to be desired more than gold.

In the Gospel story we have an example of Peter speaking unwisely and being rebuked for it. Right after a confession that Jesus is the Messiah, Peter suggested that Jesus was taking the idea too seriously. For this Peter received the most serious of reproaches: "Get behind me, Satan!" (Mark 8:33).

James provides the clearest warning about the wise and unwise use of words in his warning to us to be careful about what we say, since as teachers we can expect to be closely scrutinized. Just as a tiny rudder can steer a huge ship, so can a tiny tongue steer a person's life either toward serenity or calamity.

Story: CAN'T PUT IT BACK

This is perhaps a very common illustration for children's time. We know of a church in a small community where the practice was to have a lay person lead the children's time each Sunday. This responsibility was rotated through a list of volunteers who would prepare the talk. One particular person on the list had only one story to tell. He would tell this story every time his name came up on the rotation, so the congregation got the same illustration about twice a year. No one seemed to mind, though, as the speaker was a well-loved elderly person who just wanted to do what he could for the worship service. We sent that church a complimentary copy of Come as a Child, Book 1.

Show the children a tube of toothpaste. Start to put some on a toothbrush. Be expressive so that the children and the adults can see you are making a point by exaggeration. Put so much toothpaste on the brush that it starts to drip off the sides. Have a handkerchief or cloth on the floor to catch the drips. When one of the children points out that you have squeezed out too much toothpaste, apologize and say you can just put the extra back in. Make an effort to return the excess toothpaste. After a bit of exasperation give up and explain that once the toothpaste is out of the tube, there is no way to get it back in.

Our words are like the toothpaste. Once we have said something, there is no way we can take the words back, so we must be careful with our speech. We should be certain to say things that are good and complimentary to our family and friends. We should be certain to say things that God would be pleased to hear, because we cannot hide our words once we have spoken them. Remember when you are tempted to say something bad about someone that once you have said it, it's like squeezing too much toothpaste — we can't get it back.

Keywords

Speech

Toothpaste

Wisdom

Words

You will need:

Toothpaste

Toothbrush

Handkerchief or cloth

Proverbs
31:10-31

Psalm 1

James
3:13–4:3,
7-8a

Mark
9:30-37

Message

We do not seek glory and praise for ourselves. We just do the job that must be done for the sake of God's glory, not our own.

Commentary

For a children's story there is not much in the Proverbs description of the ideal wife. We seriously doubt any children in your church would be able to see this paragon of virtue in their own mothers. We love our wives deeply, but we do not expect them to live up to the standards of the woman described in Proverbs 31. But there is a good reference to be drawn from this chapter that is applicable to all Christians. The virtuous woman does all her Herculean tasks with no thought to glory and praise for herself. In this way the chapter has a message for us all. We should not be concerned for the thanks or the rewards we will get for our labor. We do all things for God's glory, not our own.

Psalm 1 tells us that happiness comes from finding delight in the law of the Lord and not from wasting time following ill advice or putting down others.

James reminds us that wisdom is seen in good works and breeds further good things such as peacefulness, gentleness, and mercy. Selfish ambition leads to disorder. We should not be focused on our own glory; instead, we should focus on a harvest of righteousness.

Jesus made it quite clear to the disciples that their concern over their own glory was misplaced. He drew a child into their circle and explained that by welcoming the least in his name, they would be welcoming him and God. Obviously the great and powerful were not important in Jesus' way of looking at things. Why are they so important to us?

Story: GLORY BE

Keywords

Glory

Toys

The Velveteen Rabbit

We would like to make the contrast between true glory and false or flashy glory. The best illustration along this line in the child's mind would probably be a toy. Every Christmas there is at least one toy for each age group that seems to be the "must-have" toy of the year. We can go through the list of Cabbage Patch Dolls, GI Joes, Barbies, electronic puppies, and so on. And we can think of a few popular movies that focused on a child's craving for the "must-have" toy of the time — "A Christmas Story" with Darren McGavin or "Jingle All The Way" with Arnold Schwarzenegger. A non-Christmas example would be the animated "Toy Story," either 1 or 2. A common thing about these "must-have" toys is that they all, sooner or later, end up as yesterday's news, forgotten, broken, or discarded in favor of the new fad.

We can suggest two ways to take this children's time. The Velveteen Rabbit by Margery Williams is a beautifully written tale about the false glory given to the flashy toys in a child's playroom as compared to the real value of the most loved toy. It is too long to read in a service time (we have seen this done; it was terrible), but you could become familiar with the story and then give a synopsis using cardboard props to illustrate it.

As an alternative, bring in a toy from your household or from the church nursery. Choose a toy that was obviously glorious and beautiful when new, but is now worn, broken, and useless.

You will need:
A loved toy

This toy would once have been someone's most favorite toy in the whole world, but like all things its beauty and glory have faded. If it has any glory now, it is in the fact that one day it was loved by a child, and that child remembers that love. But we are not toys to God. God's love for us never fades, even though we are worn, broken, and old.

Esther
7:1-6, 9-10;
9:20-22

Psalm 124

James
5:13-20

Mark
9:38-50

Keywords
Courage
Faith
Prayer
Prompts

Message

It is a good thing when people support and cheer for good things in our world.

Commentary

While we admit that reading the whole story of Esther for a Sunday worship would take you well into lunch time, we believe the whole story should be told. Tell the congregation that their homework is to read the whole book at home. Along with the pleasant images of a beauty contest and the triumph of the under-dog, there are disturbing images of massacre and execution. Stick to the pleasant images for the children's time, but in your own mind do not forget that the Book of Esther is a mixed bag.

Many different themes can be drawn from Esther's story, but in light of the other readings for today's lectionary, we see great potential in sticking with the theme that those who put their trust in God come out winners in the end — even if they don't know it.

Psalm 124 is a song of praise to God for God's support during times of trouble: "Our help is in the name of the LORD, who made heaven and earth" (verse 8). You can't get better support than what you get from the one who made this whole thing in the first place.

James encourages us to lay our problems before God: "The prayer of faith will save the sick, and the Lord will raise them up" (James 5:15). When the disciples encountered an unknown person using Christ's name to heal people, they were indignant. But Jesus explained that God will use others as long as they are faithful.

Story: ONCE UPON A TIME THERE WAS A BEAUTIFUL QUEEN

The story of Esther makes a great children's story to be presented in an entertaining way. This idea involves the whole congregation in telling the tale. Prepare two prompting signs to be held up at appropriate times. One sign reads "YEAH!"

*or "HURRAY!" or "APPLAUSE!" The other sign reads
"BOO!" or "YECH!" Read or recite from memory a
condensed version of the story of Esther. Hold up the signs at
appropriate times for the children and congregation. You be
the judge for those times. Our version of the story follows. As
mentioned above, you must be familiar with the whole story
in order to effectively present an abridged version.*

Once upon a time there was a beautiful queen who
lived with a loving husband, the king. Her name was
Esther. (YEAH!) Her father lived near the palace, and
they would often meet and talk about things that were hap-
pening in the kingdom. His name was Mordecai. (YEAH!)
Mordecai had done good things for the king, and the king
liked him. For example, one time some people tried to kill
the king, but Mordecai found out and warned the king in
time to save him. (YEAH!)

But there was a mean man who worked for the king.
His name was Haman. (BOO!) Haman did not like
Mordecai. Haman did not know that Mordecai was the
queen's father. They often disagreed. Haman believed that
all the people should bow down and praise him because he
worked for the king. (BOO!) Mordecai believed that only
God should be bowed down to and praised. (YEAH!)

Haman (BOO!) got so angry with Mordecai (YEAH!)
that he asked the king to make a new law. This new law
meant that anyone who did not bow down and praise Haman
would be punished. (BOO!) Mordecai and all his friends were
afraid of this new law because it meant they would all be
punished. So Mordecai asked his daughter Esther (YEAH!)
to talk to the king and get him to change the law.

Esther was afraid to talk to the king because she
thought he might get angry with her. So Esther prayed and
asked Mordecai and all his friends to pray. (YEAH!) Soon,
Esther built up enough courage to talk to the king.
(YEAH!) When she told the king about how the new law
would punish so many people, even her, the king did
become angry. But he was not angry with Esther. He was
angry with Haman. (BOO!)

Esther and Mordecai and all their friends (YEAH!)
were saved from the punishment. In the end it was Haman
(BOO!) who was punished. Because Esther and Mordecai
and all their friends were courageous and prayed for God's
help, they were saved. (YEAH!)

Job 1:1;
2:1-10

Psalm 26

Hebrews
1:1-4;
2:5-12

Mark
10:2-16

Keywords

Humans

Signs

Message

Who comes to God? Those whom God loves. And God loves God's human beings.

Commentary

God loves creation. The opening of Job shows God clearly pleased with Job and even "bragging" to Satan about him. As the story of Job progressed and Job's situation got worse, he questioned God's protection, but maintained his integrity and steadfast trust in God's overall goodness: "Shall we receive the good at the hand of God, and not receive the bad?" (Job 2:10). The writer of Psalm 26 cries to the Lord for divine help. While describing the good life he has lived, he implies that he should be deserving of God's grace. Indeed, God does love the righteous person. Does God require a person to be so upright and perfect to be worthy of God's grace?

In Hebrews the author describes his understanding of God's plan for salvation as brought about through Christ. In the passages read today we are told that humanity is created "for a little while lower than the angels" (Hebrews 2:7). In God's great scheme of creation, humans are God's pride and joy — God has "crowned them with glory and honor" (verse 7).

In the Mark passage Jesus explains God's intention for humans, first with an example of marriage and then with an example of children. It is God's intention that humans live in harmony — and God includes all humans in equal ways. This book is not the place to discuss divorce and adultery. What is striking and new about Jesus' words here is that he holds both the male and female equally responsible for their relationships. In God's eyes they are "one flesh" (verse 8). With children Jesus makes it clear that they are precious and equal in God's sight: "Whoever does not receive the kingdom of God as a little child will never enter it" (verse 15).

Story: NOT ALLOWED?

You will need a few signs that restrict access to places. Signs like "No Trespassing" or "Danger — High Voltage — Keep Out" are common, and you may even have some in your church.

One sign that would be perfect, but is rare, is one that says, "No Children Allowed." Another cute option would be a handmade sign that looks like it was taken off someone's tree fort that says, "No Girls Allowed." If you have any creative gifts, make some signs and show them to the children. Speak along these lines:

Have you ever seen signs like these around our church or our community? Signs are important around here because they can warn us not to enter a room where we might get hurt. Signs can also be disturbing, since sometimes people will put up a sign to keep people out just because they don't like them. You know that there are places around this building and around our town where we are not allowed to go. For good reasons and for bad reasons, we are not allowed to go some places; there are usually signs to tell us about these places.

Do you think you would ever see such a sign on God's door? Do you think there are any people whom God would not want in God's kingdom? I don't think so. God wants all of God's children and adults to live good lives and to be welcome in God's fellowship. Today we read a few stories about how God looks at all people the same and would never say to anyone that he or she cannot enjoy God's presence. One of the stories talks specifically about children. It tells us that God's kingdom is made up of people who are like children, and everyone can receive God's kingdom if he or she is like a child.

You will need:
Warning signs

21st Sunday After Pentecost

Message

Everyone wants to be understood for who he or she is. Even if no one else sees you for who you are, God sees, understands, and loves you.

Commentary

Poor Job. He wanted desperately to find God and to plead his case before God, for surely God would heed Job's reasoning. Job cried out as we all do, pleading to be understood, if

Job 23:1-9, 16-17

Psalm 22:1-15

Hebrews 4:12-16

Mark 10:17-31

only he could lay his case before God. Job spoke for all humanity in wanting to understand and to be understood.

The passage in Hebrews gives assurance that God does understand us, if only too well. God sees in us and through us; nothing is hidden. But we have an advocate in Jesus, who thoroughly understands our weaknesses and what it means to be tempted. We know we can find mercy and grace because Jesus "has been there."

Jesus' understanding and his role in our life is not confined to the hereafter, as we read in the Gospel of Mark. He understands us in the here and now. When Jesus was approached by the young man, the inquirer was seeking to understand and to be understood. He really wanted to know what he must do to attain eternal life. Jesus looked at him and loved him. Jesus understood. His response was to the point. Jesus identified the one area in his life where he must change. This was not said out of spite or anger; it was a loving admonition that this is what he must do to inherit the eternal life he craves. God sees and understands us. And often God gives us just as pointed a response to our requests for answers. And when we don't get the answers we're looking for, well, you get the picture.

Story: SAY CHEESE

Have a camera prepared to take a picture. Instant-developing cameras are great for this because the kids can see the picture by the end of the story. Bring along an x-ray picture as well. Speak to them along these lines:

You're such a fine-looking bunch of kids, I want to remember this moment forever. Now let's get everyone all set up. (*Take a generous amount of time to set up the portrait. Do it right and make it look good. You want them to understand that this is important for you to get a good picture of them. When you're ready, snap the picture.*) **That was great. Now I know exactly who was here this morning and what you're all like. What are some of the things I will know when I look at the picture?** (*Help them with their answers if they need it; point out hair styles, teeth missing, clothes, and so forth.*) **But that picture will only tell me what the outside of you is like; it won't tell me what the inside of you is like. To do that I would need a big camera called an x-ray machine. It takes pictures like this.** (*Show them the x-ray.*) **It sees right through your clothes, your skin, your**

muscles, and can even see your bones. But if I had an x-ray machine, I could only see what's inside of you, like bones and things. I wouldn't see what's really inside you. A doctor might use an x-ray to see if you were hurt, if you had a broken bone or something. It can't take pictures of your thoughts and your feelings, though; those are things that only you know — well, only you and God.

The Bible tells us that God knows what we're thinking and feeling, and that's a good thing. Just like I will use this picture to tell me what you look like, and like a doctor uses an x-ray to know if you're hurt, God looks into your thoughts and feelings to know if you're hurt too. God wants to understand why you feel the way you do, and God wants to help. So every time you smile for a camera or have an x-ray taken, remember that God knows what goes on in your heart. That makes me feel good, because it's good to know that someone understands me.

22nd Sunday After Pentecost

Message

We all have to ask questions to get information we need. Sometimes knowing the right question is most of the answer.

Job 38:1-7, (34-41)

Psalm 104:1-9, 24, 35c

Hebrews 5:1-10

Mark 10:35-45

Commentary

Throughout the Book of Job, Job had been crying to God for an answer as to why these calamities had come upon him. Now in Chapter 38 the story flips, and it's God's turn to ask the questions. And boy did God ever give Job an earful. For the next two chapters Job was barraged with rhetorical questions about the nature of God and humans and who has any right to question God's way in doing things. The fact is, we all question God's wisdom when things have gone poorly for us. But when we take a read through these two chapters, we can't help but feel a little bit petty about our silly concerns. The tactic worked for Job, as we see in Chapter 42 that Job realized his place and apologized, using some of God's own words from today's passage.

Psalm 104 supports God's sovereignty claim by recognizing God as creator and sustainer of the earth.

In the Gospel story we have an example of the wrong questions to ask. James and John approached Jesus and opened their request, asking him to grant it even before it is asked. Jesus returned with a question of what it is they want before promising anything. After all, with the way the Sons of Thunder usually acted, it was only prudent not to commit oneself unwittingly. When they asked for special places at Jesus' side, he responded with, "You do not know what you are asking" (Mark 10:38).

What questions do we ask of God? Are they the good questions, the right questions? Are they questions sincerely trying to understand our relationship with him, or do we often ask questions just for our own gain?

You will need:
Candy

Keywords
Candy
Questions

Story: TWENTY QUESTIONS

It's all about the questions we ask. Play a game of Twenty Questions. Have a bag of goodies of some sort. Shake the bag a bit to make some sound. Tell the children they have to play a game of Twenty Questions if they want to have what's in the bag. You will only answer yes or no to each of their questions. If and when they guess what it is, they may have it. You can make this as difficult or as easy as you wish, depending on the children.

It is important in this game that you ask the right questions, just as it is important in our faith to always be willing to ask the right questions of our parents, our minister, and our teachers in order for us to understand more about God. When Jesus was a very young boy, not much older than any of you, he spent a couple of days in the church and was asking the elders all sorts of questions about God and faith. They were amazed that he asked such important questions. You can try to amaze the older people in our church with the questions you ask us about faith and God.

23rd Sunday After Pentecost

Message

In the big things and the small things, God should be worshiped and thanked.

Commentary

Job is a hard character upon which to base a pleasant children's story. The whole book must be read at some point in every Christian's life as it raises all sorts of issues without, we feel, really resolving them. We believe the Job story is in the Bible as one of the many for which there is no clearcut moral or answer; instead, we are expected to wrestle with reaching our own conclusions about what God wants us to know. The passage we deal with for this Sunday, though, may at least be summarized as this: It was not until Job acknowledged the sovereignty of God and humbled himself before God's majesty that he was restored to health and wholeness. We have to accept that humanity is not the pinnacle of existence; God is. In humility we are able to accomplish far more than in arrogance.

The psalmist recognizes this. Psalm 34:2 suggests it is the humble who hear God and are glad for it.

The Hebrews passage dwells on the superiority of Christ as a priest to intercede for us with God. None of the "former" priests can do what Christ can do for us.

When Jesus healed Bartimaeus in Mark, he gave a reason for this miracle to be possible. "Your faith has made you well," said Jesus (Mark 10:52). If Bartimaeus had not acknowledged the divinity of Jesus, would Jesus have been able to do anything for him? Perhaps, because God can do whatever God wants. We have stories where faith in God was not a requirement for Christ's healing. But in this story it is plain that faith — not shouting or springing up and running to Jesus, but simply faith — had made the man well.

In our lives, how good are we at acknowledging the power, action, and grace of God the Father, Christ the Savior, and the Holy Spirit? Let's do it more often and give thanks.

Job 42:1-6, 10-17

Psalm 34:1-8, (19-22)

Hebrews 7:23-28

Mark 10:46-52

Keywords
Graces
Humility
Prayers
Snacks

Story: GOD IS GREAT, GOD IS GOOD

Have some healthy snack foods ready, such as apples or granola bars.

This story depends on the simple practice of saying grace before meals. We sense that this tradition is not as prominent in our society as it used to be. We know of many churchgoing families that just don't take the time to return thanks before their family meals. Our lives are rushed and hectic. Praying to God out loud seems to be difficult for people, even when it is with our loved ones. We'd like to challenge church people to take this simple thing seriously. In praying before each meal we accomplish a few things. It draws family together. It slows things down. Most importantly, though, in returning thanks before each meal, we are confessing our belief in God as superior to us. We are admitting that even though we worked hard to earn the money to put this food on the table, we know we would have nothing were it not for the grace of God. Give thanks.

Ask the children if they do anything special each mealtime before they start eating. Some of them will mention that they say a grace. Ask them to repeat that grace if they are comfortable with doing so. This may unsettle others, including parents in the pews who realize this is a practice they have strayed away from. We say it's OK to unsettle people in church — Jesus sure did. But be careful not to focus on any child or family that does not participate in this. It's not the child's fault if graces are not said at home. There is no need to embarrass anyone in church.

Explain the importance of giving thanks to God for all the wonderful things we have, and especially that each day we get enough food to see us through. Teach the children this simple grace that many of them will already know:

God is great, God is good,
Let us thank him for this food. Amen.

After saying this together give each child a healthy snack food, such as an apple or a granola bar.

You will need:
Snack food

Keywords
Love
Mirror

Message

As we try to be good Christians by loving God and our neighbor, do not forget that God expects us to love ourselves also.

Ruth
1:1-18

Psalm 146

Hebrews
9:11-14

Mark
12:28-34

Commentary

Ruth's story involves a lot of love. Naomi showed love for her daughters-in-law by freeing them to return home, even though this would have left her on her own. Ruth showed love by steadfastly clinging to Naomi; the poem Ruth recites to convince Naomi is one of the most romantic passages in the Bible. It spills over with love. Then the rest of the story of Ruth uses love as the theme that moves God's people. We believe Ruth must have been strongly self-assured and confident in herself in order to stay with Naomi and travel to a foreign land.

When dealing with the Great Commandment as read in Mark 12 and the other Gospels, we always point out that the love of God and the love of our neighbors is connected to the love of ourself. Our love for God and for others is not of much value if we are not confident in our love for ourselves.

Story: MIRRORS

Ask the children to name a few people whom they love. They will likely respond with mom and dad and family. Maybe someone will mention a close friend or a pet. It is unlikely that any of them will mention themselves.

Hold a mirror up to them and ask if any one of them loves this person.

It is important for us to remember that God calls us to love God and to love our neighbor, but it is equally important that we love ourselves. We are able to love ourselves because even though we may have done wrong things or thought bad thoughts before, God forgives us, says it's OK, and tells us to try not to do it again.

You will need:
Mirror (one large enough for several people to look into, or several smaller mirrors so each child can have his or her own)

Ruth 3:1-5;
4:13-17

Psalm 127

Hebrews
9:24-28

Mark
12:38-44

Message

Sometimes our belief in Christ's good news means that we will have to take some risks to make his love real in the world.

Commentary

The whole story of Ruth should be read on occasion, but it is hard to fit the whole book into a church service. The snippets we get in the lectionary are good, but nothing compares to reading it with all its subtleties and images. In this small section we see the result of Ruth's courageous risk in staying with Naomi. She had to risk more in order to secure her future with Boaz, such as sneaking into the workers camp to be beside him during the evening. As a result of her risk, though, Boaz was convinced he wished to marry her. From their marriage was born the grandfather of King David. Not only was Ruth and Naomi's future secured, but things were also set in place for the security of the whole nation of Israel.

When Jesus saw a widow put two small copper coins into the treasury, he knew how much it was costing her; and he praised her for it. She courageously risked her meager savings so that other people's lives might be better. This showed God's love at work through her.

Think of the risk God took in the sacrifice of God's only son. The Hebrews passage explains how Christ's death by his own blood is much more powerful than the old sacrifices that the priests did. It was not their blood being spilled in the Temple sacrifices. They were not risking anything. What are we willing to give up so that God's love will be seen in the world?

The Twenty-Fifth Sunday After Pentecost usually falls near November 11 — the day set aside in North America and other areas as Remembrance Day, known as Veterans Day in the United States. This is a time to remember the risks taken by many people in our past century in order to secure our freedoms. Many people died; their blood was spilled. At a time of remembrance of past sacrifices, it is good to ask ourselves what we are willing to risk to ensure God's love is supreme in the world and never again will we go to war.

Story: THE POPPY

Hold some poppy flowers in your hand — either live flowers or the artificial ones distributed by the veterans. Tell the children the story of the poppy.

You will need:
Poppy

The poppy has been a symbol of remembrance for those who died in wars since the time of Napoleon and Wellington. It was noticed that fields that were bare before a battle came forth with the blood-red flowers after the fighting ended. A connection was made between the color of the flowers and the blood of the casualties. The poppy became famous for this when Col. John McCrae, a Canadian doctor, wrote the poem "In Flanders Fields" after a battle during the First World War. (*If it is not used in your memorial service, this would be a good time to read "In Flanders Fields."*) Over the next few years people working in hospitals and other services began wearing a poppy in memory of people who died in battle.

Explain to the children that this is the Sunday where we remember that many people died in wars in the past century. Since the 1920s people have been pinning a poppy on their coats or shirts this time of year. This is a symbol we use to remember that so many people risked and even lost their lives in terrible wars.

We all know that wars are terrible things and cause terrible suffering for people. We also know that God does not want any people to suffer in God's creation. God created things to be good and to support human life. In the Bible stories we read today, there are people who took big risks to make things better for the world. One woman risked ridicule and rejection to help out her mother-in-law. Another woman who was very poor sacrificed most of her money to help out other people. These people risked and sacrificed to make things better.

Keywords
Peace
Poppy
Remembrance
Risk
Sacrifice

We will remember people who risked and sacrificed their lives in war to make things better. But when we look at the poppy as a symbol of remembrance, we should also use it as a symbol of our promise to make sure we live lovingly so that wars will not be fought in the future. What will you do, or what will you risk, or what will you give up in order to keep peace in your family, neighborhood, or school?

1 Samuel
1:4-20

Psalm 16

Hebrews
10:11-14,
(15-18),
19-25

Mark
13:1-8

Keywords

Change
Light bulbs

Message

We do not seek glory and praise for ourselves. We just do the job that must be done for the sake of God's glory, not our own.

Commentary

With the exception of the psalm this Sunday's readings all dwell on necessary changes. In First Samuel we get the story of the beginnings of the prophet Samuel's life. His mother, although happily married, was barren and because of this was tormented by her husband's other wife. Despite the fact that her husband loved her dearly, Hannah was unfulfilled and miserable without a child. She knew this had to change and prayed fervently — so fervently that the priest mistook her for a drunk and chided her.

The understanding of Christ in Hebrews is that he is superior to any salvation avenue of the past. It seems that God understood that God's relationship with the Jews was not working out; so God made the change, offering Christ as the final sacrifice and making all other sacrifices unnecessary. This change in God's offer of salvation has made salvation possible for all of us.

In Mark Jesus predicts that a great change is about to come. The Temple worship, so important to the Jews, would be overturned and made obsolete. He may have been talking predictively about the destruction of the Temple a few decades later, but we believe he was indicating that the form of worship these buildings and stones represented would soon be no more.

In Psalm 16 the singer seems to be blessed with everything he needs. For one whose life and work is focused on the Lord, there seems to be no need for any change.

Story: MAKING A CHANGE

An easy illustration for the theme of change is a lamp. Have a table lamp with a burned-out bulb in it and an extra light bulb handy. Place the lamp high enough for everyone to see it, even at the back of the church. When you turn the switch, it does not come on. Point out that it is plugged in, and it was working fine earlier today. What could be wrong now? One of the children will know that the bulb needs changing. Unplug the lamp, change the bulb, replug the lamp, and turn the switch. The light will come on.

When we know there is something wrong with something as simple as a lamp, we know we have to change something to get it back to being good for us. There are times in our families, and in our neighborhoods, when we know things are not working. We know that something should be better than it actually is, and so we know that we must change something. Ask yourself what things you know are not working now and what you know you should try to change.

Jesus Christ asked people to realize that they must make a big change in the way they worship God and in the way they treat one another. He taught us ways to be good and supportive to everyone, and he challenged us to be brave enough to change things so that life would be good for everyone.

You will need:
Lamp

Burned-out light bulb

Spare light bulb

27th Sunday After Pentecost

Message

There are leaders in the world, in our community, and in our church. Our leaders are best when they focus their leadership on God's will.

Commentary

David's reign as king was ending when the poem he speaks in today's passage is recorded. It sounds very much like one of his psalms and could easily have been included in that book. The story of David's kingship is long, with many elements and incidents. His story and the glory of his kingdom shaped Jewish history for the rest of recorded time. Was David

2 Samuel 23:1-7

Psalm 132:1-12

Revelation 1:4b-8

John 18:33-37

105

a good king? The verdict is mixed. He did many great and glorious things that his descendants are proud to remember. In remembrance, though, we cannot escape the truth that many of his acts were abusive, cruel, and inappropriate. On the whole, how do we determine if someone is a good leader or not?

Psalm 132 is a song attributed to David on the occasion of one of his glorious deeds: having the Ark of the Covenant moved into Jerusalem. The Lordship of God is outlined in the Revelation passage. God is acknowledged as the supreme ruler — the true ruler of the universe. God is "ruler of the kings of the earth" (verse 5) and "the Alpha and the Omega . . . the Almighty" (verse 8).

In John, Jesus and Pilate discussed kingship and leadership. Notice that Pilate, surrounded by the trappings of leadership and authority, seems small in the presence of Christ. Christ's authority and lordship do not depend on human constructions, but come from a power far greater than anything we can create on earth.

This Sunday is always in November, the month when our American readers go to the polls each four years to elect leadership for their nation. In Ontario, Canada, our home, municipal elections are always held in November. This is a good time to discuss leadership from a faith perspective.

Keywords
Election
Leaders
Kings

Story: WHO'S THE BOSS OF ME NOW?

Every child knows that someone in his or her life has authority over him or her. There is someone in every child's life who is making decisions for that child, leading and teaching him or her the right things to say and do. We believe this to be true of every adult too, but sometimes in our pride we are reluctant to confess this. This storytime works to draw out the children's awareness of good, faith-centered leadership.

Bring along some election paraphernalia — buttons, hats, posters, or anything promoting a local candidate or elected official. Show these to the children and explain what they are. Some of the children may be aware of what elections are and why items like these show up from time to time in the community.

Ask the children if anyone knows who the local elected leader is. Do they know who the mayor is or the governor, prime minister, or president? Children are not taking part in elections and do not have much awareness of these things, but they will have a vague idea that every now and then their family and community gets a little caught up in the democratic process. Older children in the group will have been studying these matters at school and may be quite proud to say they know who these leaders are.

Do the children know how these leaders are selected? Explain in very simple terms how your local elections operate.

Next, ask the children who is in charge of their home. Who is in charge at their school or at the church school? These are questions that will draw in the younger children because they all know that someone other than themselves is a leader in these places. Ask the children if they know how these people became leaders. In most cases there has not been an election. In the case of the family, leadership is established according to presence and experience in the home. In school, leaders are chosen based upon academic achievement and professional qualifications. All of our churches have different methods for choosing leaders, but one consistent element is prayerful searching for God's will in our church leadership.

There are leaders and teachers throughout our lives. Some of them are very good, and some are not very good. It is hard for us to know who is a good leader and who is not until we have been with him or her for a long time. One thing that we learn from many of our Bible stories is that leaders are always better leaders when they realize that they, themselves, have leaders more important than they are. Leaders who know there are more important leaders know that the leader of all leaders is God. Leaders who believe this and guide their people with this in mind are always the best leaders of all. We should always be searching for and selecting leaders who know this simple truth.

A good alternative illustration for this story is found in Pentecost 3b (page 64).

A good alternative illustration for this story is found in Pentecost 3b (page 64).

> **You will need:**
> Election
> paraphernalia

INDEXES

INDEX OF SCRIPTURES -- YEAR B

INDEX

EPISTLES

NDEX

GOSPELS

INDEX OF KEYWORDS - YEAR B